Volume I
STRATEGIC PLANNING
AND THE MBO PROCESS

MANAGEMENT BY OBJECTIVES

A SELF-INSTRUCTIONAL APPROACH

MANAGEMENT BY OBJECTIVES
A SELF-INSTRUCTIONAL APPROACH

WILLIAM C. GIEGOLD
Virginia Polytechnic Institute and State University

Volume I
STRATEGIC PLANNING AND THE MBO PROCESS

McGRAW-HILL BOOK COMPANY

New York / St. Louis / San Francisco / Auckland / Bogotá / Düsseldorf
Johannesburg / London / Madrid / Mexico / Montreal / New Delhi / Panama
Paris / São Paulo / Singapore / Sydney / Tokyo / Toronto

Library of Congress Cataloging in Publication Data

Giegold, William C
    Management by objectives.

     CONTENTS: v. 1. Strategic planning.
     1. Management by objectives—Collected works.
I. Title.
HD30.12.G53   658.4   78–14764
ISBN 0-07-023192-3

STRATEGIC PLANNING AND THE MBO PROCESS
Volume I

MANAGEMENT BY OBJECTIVES: A Self-Instructional Approach

 234567890 DODO 7832109

This book was set in Univers by Allen Wayne Technical Corp.
The editors were Robert G. Manley, John Hendry, Bob Leap, and M. Susan Norton;
the designer was Anne Canevari Green;
the production supervisor was Jeanne Selzam.
The drawings were done by Allen Wayne Technical Corp.
R. R. Donnelley & Sons Company was printer and binder.

CONTENTS

v

PREFACE

This is the first volume of a three-volume series entitled *Management by Objectives: A Self-Instructional Approach.* The series is intended to achieve the following objectives:

1. To facilitate one's understanding of the management system known as Management by Objectives, or MBO for short.
2. To identify and describe the elements which make up the MBO system and the interpersonal skills which enhance the chances of its successful implementation.
3. To give the reader an opportunity to develop the required skills and to experience some of the problems and pitfalls that may arise in implementing MBO.
4. To help the reader develop a management system which can adapt the general principles of MBO to the specific needs of his or her organization.

Each volume may be used independently of the others by those readers or organizations whose needs lie predominantly in the areas covered by only one or two of the books. In this volume we cover the strategic planning process, as described below. Volume II concentrates on the processes of setting objectives and formulating action plans, while Volume III deals with performance appraisal.

The three volumes are self-instructional since they allow an individual reader, by completing the exercises, to apply the principles of MBO to his or her own organization or job, and thus have a first-hand knowledge of the problems and pitfalls one may encounter when introducing MBO into an organization. If you are a manager, completion of this self-study will give you the ability and confidence to install such a system in your own component, with little or no outside assistance. The *Leader's Manual* which accompanies the series gives further help to any reader who takes on the responsibility of conducting MBO training for others in an organization — employees or coworkers — in a group setting.

This volume, like each of the others in the series, begins with a general overview of the MBO system. It then turns to the organizational structuring and planning activities which are so important in determining whether or not MBO produces *results.* The two primary benefits to the organization from the "total MBO" approach consist of improvements in the *behavioral* and the *structural* areas. Together these provide the full effects of an MBO system. The participative or behavioral emphasis, if imposed by itself on an organization in which the structural groundwork has not been carefully prepared, is not likely to achieve the full potential of MBO. On the other hand, complete concentration on "straightening out" the organization — defining its mission, dividing the areas of responsibility, writing clear job descriptions, staffing for technical competence, etc. — may also prevent one from reaching full potential for organizational effectiveness.

The history of management is filled with dramatic turnaround stories in which a new management concentrates its efforts on reestablishing a firm sense of direction, setting up standards, and bringing in new talent. The MBO approach facilitates this type of management action, using the principles described in this volume. However, don't stop with Volume I. As you proceed through Volumes II (*Objective Setting*) and III (*Performance Appraisal*), you will find an increasing emphasis on the "people" aspects of MBO. Neglecting the vital human element will leave your organization far short of its potential, although it may be completely straightened out and turned around. Our ultimate objective in this series is to provide you with the skills not only to turn it around, but also to "turn it on." For the moment, however, we will concentrate on straightening things out.

In this volume we will work on (1) clarifying the purpose of your organization, (2) analyzing its strengths and weaknesses, (3) defining individual responsibilities, (4) establishing standards and measurements of performance, and, perhaps most important of all, (5) selecting the areas of effort which will receive top priority in terms of time and other resources; for as Peter Drucker has said, the truly effective organization is not one which merely does things right. There must also be the assurance that the right things are being done. Or, as an executive we worked with in installing a successful MBO system said in announcing the purpose of the effort to his managers at the start of an implementation conference, "We're here to make sure that we do the *right* things *well*."

There is nothing in the objective-setting process per se to ensure that the "right things" have been selected. However, strategic planning will improve the selection process. Hence, our deliberate delay in introducing the admittedly important and difficult task of writing objectives. If you are anxious about that phase of MBO, feel free to browse through Volume II, but we urge you to spend an adequate amount of time on the painstaking and, to some people, unexciting work contained in this volume on planning. If you are like most good managers, you are probably very action-oriented, and may even regard planning as something best left to the staff specialist while you get on with the job. However, no matter what level of leadership you occupy in your organization, an important part of that leadership involves the things you will be practicing in this volume. A high level of activity is important, but unless that activity is oriented and continually reoriented to the needs of your changing environment, you are in danger of falling into the "activity trap" — a state in which you may be doing many things extremely well, but falling far short of the definition of true effectiveness.

No book in a field as broad as management is the work of the writer alone. We acknowledge the immense contributions of those previous authors whose works are cited herein, as well as those unnamed whose thoughts provided the springboard for this work. A special debt of gratitude is due Mike Crump of Syracuse University's School of Management, who conceived the idea for this series but who unfortunately was unable to play his rightful role in making it come to pass.

We thank consultants Frank Mahoney and Art Kirn, and C. C. Schmidt, for their painstaking reviews of the manuscript and their helpful suggestions, many of which they will find incorporated within. Project manager John Hendry has shown great patience and skill in keeping the author's feet on the ground. They and the McGraw-Hill staff — Bob Manley, Bob Leap, Anne Green, and the many copy editors, artists, compositors, and others who have put a bit of themselves into these books — would command any author's admiration and respect.

Finally, to Irma, who typed the manuscripts and whose editing of the raw material made the job much easier for the professionals, goes more than thanks for her loving support throughout.

William C. Giegold

Volume I
STRATEGIC PLANNING AND THE MBO PROCESS

MANAGEMENT BY OBJECTIVES
A SELF-INSTRUCTIONAL APPROACH

UNIT 1

INTRODUCTION

AN OVERVIEW OF THE MANAGEMENT BY OBJECTIVES SYSTEM

The phrase "management by objectives," or MBO for short, has become a part of the language of management throughout the world. Managers, supervisors, and others in responsible positions at every level in almost every type and size of organization, from churches to the military, and from the multinational corporation to the family-owned hardware store, are on speaking acquaintance with the concept. It has appeared under several names — results-oriented management, management by objectives and results (MBO/R), work planning and review, "planagement," and management by agreement, to list a few. The names reveal the particular emphasis or bias of their authors. One stresses the planning aspects. Another emphasizes the give-and-take by which bosses and subordinates agree on their mutual goals. Others reflect merely their authors' dissatisfaction with the ability of the original name — MBO — to convey the full meaning and purpose of the management system to which it refers.

Whatever its title, the principles of this system remain the same, as valid as they were when originally proposed a quarter of a century ago. They compose the most rational system of "total management" yet developed. In spite of this, unfortunately, the potential of the system remains today largely as promise rather than realization. The ranks of those who have "tried it" in a superficial or halfhearted way and been disappointed far outnumber those who have understood it and had the will to submit to its demands. Those who have done so can testify to its merits. They can also testify to the fact that it is a *demanding* system of management.

In this guided tour of the system we will stop frequently and let you experience for yourself the extent of the commitment you must make to excellence in the profession of management when you opt for MBO. Whether you are the top person in your organization, a first-line manager, or not yet appointed to your first management job—and whether or not your organization formally adopts an MBO system—you can become a much more effective manager by putting to work on the job what you practice in this series of books.

A DEFINITION OF MANAGE-MENT BY OBJECTIVES

"Management by objectives" has been defined by George Odiorne, as:

> ❝ . . .a management process *whereby the supervisor and the subordinate, operating under a* clear definition of *the common* goals *and* priorities *of the organization established by* top management, jointly *identify the individual's major* areas of responsibility *in terms of the* results expected *of him or her, and* use *these* measures *as guides for operating the unit and assessing the* contributions *of each of its members.*[1] ❞

Written in the early days of MBO, this definition has retained its currency and covers very concisely the essential features of this system of management. It is rich in meanings which do not reveal them-

---

[1]George S. Odiorne, *Management by Objectives: A System of Managerial Leadership* (New York: Pitman, 1965), pp. 55-56.

selves until it has been examined word for word. We have emphasized several key words and phrases, and point out their significance below. In this volume and the others in this series, we will expand on each of these points to provide a thorough knowledge of the principles of MBO and how to put them to work in your organization. We will also relate them to your effectiveness as an individual, on and off the job.

The key words are these:

process— MBO, like management itself, is a continuing activity, not a "campaign," a "program," or a onetime installation project which when completed can produce results on its own. It is an endless cyclical group of interrelated management activities embodying all the conventional management functions of planning, organizing, directing, and controlling. We show it as a flowchart in Fig. 1, and will explain the steps later in this unit.

clear definition of goals— This is the thrust which the name MBO implies. Clearly defined goals or objectives provide the focus of effort which is required for the most efficient use of resources. ("Goal" and "objective" are interchangeable terms. We will primarily use the latter throughout this series.)

priorities— Objectives are not enough to ensure organizational or individual effectiveness. One must be sure that the most important objectives are tackled first, and a system for establishing priorities is a vital link in the overall process.

top management— If the clear definition of goals and priorities begins at the very top, the system achieves its fullest potential, since all parts of the organization set their sights on the same overall target. Top management also plays a continuing role in emphasizing the need for organizational improvement. The single strongest motivating factor in a successful MBO system is top management's support of and demand for the degree of management effort required by MBO.

jointly— In the MBO effort, the process of joint objective setting by the manager and the employee is the key to obtaining full cooperation and acceptance by employees. This same process is also the means by which the full knowledge and creative potential of the employee are brought to bear on the improvement needs of the organization.

areas of responsibility— Every position or job must exist for a purpose well defined in relationship to the needs of the organization. This relationship is established through the *key results areas* (KRAs) of the organization, which determine the job responsibilities most important to overall needs, and guide the search for meaningful objectives. (We will have more to say about key results areas in due course.)

results expected— The apparent emphasis on objectives in MBO may seem to neglect the purpose for which the whole effort is designed: *to produce results which would not otherwise be achieved.* Stating the expectations of management is a most potent way of communicating with employees. Expressing these expectations in terms of the needed results replaces vague exhortations or, worse yet, the silence which communicates management's acceptance of the status quo.

use ("to use," an *active* verb) — The establishment of objectives at all levels in an organization is an important part of the MBO system, but in too many cases it has been mistaken for the *purpose* of the system. A campaign is mounted, individuals and managers at all levels strain

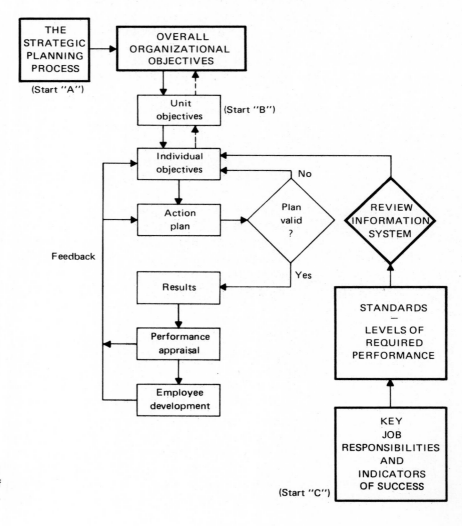

FIGURE 1
A flowchart of
the MBO process.

mightily to produce volume upon volume of objectives — and the results are placed on the shelf, to be removed only to demonstrate proudly that "we have MBO."

measures — Unless the objectives are *used* to measure progress and the measurements are then used to make adjustments and corrections which *accelerate* progress, MBO remains static and sterile, rather than becoming the dynamic and productive system it is designed to be.

contributions — MBO encourages the contributions of every individual to the overall objectives of the organization, measures each contribution, and provides the basis for rewards in proportion.

THE PURPOSE OF MBO: IMPROVED EFFECTIVENESS

A key word left out of Odiorne's description, and the primary reason for considering MBO for your organization, is "improvement." What we are working on here is improvement in both organizational and individual effectiveness. The most productive way to look at an objective is as an *improvement need* relative to the situation as it is now or as it is forecast to become unless deliberate action is taken. We stress this word and this concept of an objective because of the tendency to set objectives which merely document what the organization is already doing. Such an approach may satisfy all the formalities, but it turns MBO into a ritual rather than a thrust toward improvement.

A second reason for considering MBO, as we have suggested, is that it provides guidance in the conduct of the management process itself. As a framework for organizing managerial thought and activity, MBO satisfies all the needs of a manager who is attempting to follow the prescriptions of management authorities such as Peter

It is important to resist the tendency to set objectives which merely document what the organization is already doing. (© Brilliant Enterprises, 1974.)

TO BE SURE
OF HITTING
THE TARGET,

SHOOT FIRST

AND, WHATEVER YOU HIT,
CALL IT THE TARGET.

Drucker. Drucker's concept of the management job requires first answering the question: "What are the purposes and nature of our organization, and what should they be?" Next, clear objectives and goals are established, with priorities and measures of performance. Then a climate is created in which employees exercise self-correction and self-control by maintaining a continuing audit of the results and the objectives themselves, and adjusting their efforts as needed.

The correspondence between Odiorne's definition of MBO and Drucker's summary of the total management job is striking. It identifies MBO as a *system of management* rather than, in the view often taken, as a management tool or technique to be superimposed on "everything else that we are already doing."

THE MBO SYSTEM: A BRIEF DESCRIPTION

Figure 1 illustrates the system in flowchart form. The highlighted portions, strategic planning and setting organizational objectives, are covered in this first volume of the three-volume series. Volume II deals with the objective-setting, validation, and action-planning processes; Vol. III is devoted to performance appraisal.

Here, step by step, is how the whole thing works:

The strategic planning activity MBO does not "start with objectives," but with strategic planning. (See starting point A in Fig. 1.) This process is necessary to determine what kinds of objectives are compatible with the purposes, strengths, and resources of the organization. Before attempting to set organizational objectives, strategic planning answers two major questions: "Why are we here?" and "Who are we?" Only after these questions have been answered can we intelligently ask the third question: "Where are we going?" Answering the first two questions involves self-analysis by the organization, competitive and environmental analysis, and a series of comparisons—with *competitors' achievements* and with *our own potential*—to determine organizational strengths and weaknesses. This analysis, initiated by top management, determines how resources can best be concentrated and deployed, a maneuver we call "strategy selection." Strategic planning and its use in selecting organizational objectives, then, are the subject of this volume.

Although strategic planning is initiated by top management for the organization as a whole, the type of thinking it entails is equally important for a smaller component of the organization, and even for the individual employee or manager. We will discuss at several points later in this volume how these principles can be applied to a person's job or career strategy.

Overall organizational objectives   These are the short-range and long-range targets for organizational improvement established by the highest level of management. They are the basis for much of the objective setting done at lower levels in the organization, as each unit or component determines its contribution to the overall objective.

Overall organizational objectives, like all objectives in the MBO system, have three main purposes. These are to:

1.   Function as records of commitments made by their authors
2.   Serve as a yardstick for measuring progress
3.   Act as positive motivators of achievement

To be fully functional, an objective must be prepared with a number of stringent requirements continually in mind. Some of the more obvious are clarity, specificity, measurability, and surprisingly perhaps, achievability. High-sounding, ambitious objectives that exceed their author's capability, resources, or authority weaken an MBO system by destroying its credibility. We will cover the requirements of sound objectives later in this unit.

Unit objectives   All units are called on to contribute to the organization's objectives, as noted above. This does not mean, however, that the component must wait to be directed, nor does it mean that the component cannot initiate objectives based on the firsthand view of the situation which only its members enjoy. The reverse (dashed) arrow in Fig. 1 signifies the unit's influence on the overall organizational objectives and its responsibility to feed its firsthand knowledge into the system.

While the strategic planning process is the ideal starting point (A on the flowchart) for an organization adopting an MBO system, a single unit may be used as the starting point for a pilot effort (point

B). If this alternative is taken, there is still a need to assure conformance with overall organizational needs, and to think strategically about the resource deployment of the unit before deciding on its objectives.

Individual objectives   On the flowchart (Fig. 1) individual objectives are the focal point for much of the flow of information and action in the MBO process. The individual is the ultimate contributor to overall organizational objectives as well as to unit objectives. Some situations call for team objectives to which a number of persons — perhaps working for more than one manager — contribute. Ultimately, however, the contribution of each team member is an individual objective, and a matter for discussion between the employee and the manager. While we do not intend to minimize the demands of project management nor the importance of team leadership skills, we have chosen to concentrate our attention on the individual employee-manager relationship. Note that, as the reverse arrow indicates, the individual also has the opportunity and the responsibility to shape and modify the higher-level objectives. Later in this unit we will describe the other flows which terminate in this block of the diagram.

Figure 2 illustrates how the individual responds to an overall need for profit improvement in a multilevel organization. As the overall targets are considered at successively lower levels, the resulting objectives will normally become much more detailed and narrower in scope.

Note that the arrows depicting the flow of the objective-setting process point in both directions. This indicates the dynamic nature of the process, in which the ideas responding to the overall need flow *up,* while the motivating force for the generation of the nature and size of the total contributions needed flows *down.* The upward flow also implies that the total of manufacturing and other functional contributions must be examined closely against the overall need in order to determine the adequacy of the overall cost reduction effort. For example, if all individual and subfunctional manufacturing contributions only add up to $450,000 of cost reduction available in 19__ from manufacturing, the manufacturing objective itself must be reexamined.

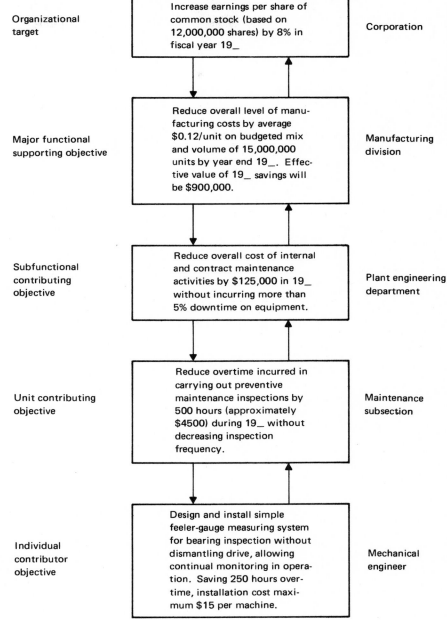

Organizational
target

Increase earnings per share of
common stock (based on
12,000,000 shares) by 8% in
fiscal year 19_

Corporation

Major functional
supporting objective

Reduce overall level of manufacturing costs by average
$0.12/unit on budgeted mix
and volume of 15,000,000
units by year end 19_. Effective value of 19_ savings will
be $900,000.

Manufacturing
division

Subfunctional
contributing
objective

Reduce overall cost of internal
and contract maintenance
activities by $125,000 in 19_
without incurring more than
5% downtime on equipment.

Plant engineering
department

Unit contributing
objective

Reduce overtime incurred in
carrying out preventive
maintenance inspections by
500 hours (approximately
$4500) during 19_ without
decreasing inspection
frequency.

Maintenance
subsection

FIGURE 2
The increasing detail
and narrowing scope of
supporting objectives in
a five-layer
organization.

Individual
contributor
objective

Design and install simple
feeler-gauge measuring system
for bearing inspection without
dismantling drive, allowing
continual monitoring in operation. Saving 250 hours overtime, installation cost maximum $15 per machine.

Mechanical
engineer

It is also possible, however, that the corporate profit-improvement target was set without enough thought as to its achievability, or that it relies too heavily on cost reduction rather than on sales volume, pricing, and other contributors to profit improvement. We will have more to say about how overall organizational objectives are set as we discuss the strategic planning process.

Plan for action   As we will stress further in Vol. II, the detailed plan for reaching an objective is an essential part of the objective itself. It details who is going to do what, when, and with whose help. The plan fulfills three important functions: it describes how the objective will be reached and therefore enhances the validity and credibility of the objective, it budgets the time and other resources required of those responsible, and it is used for monitoring progress toward the ultimate objective.

Validity of the action plan   Close scrutiny of the action plan itself is one of the best methods for validating an objective — that is, for assuring that it has a high probability of achievement. Such scrutiny determines whether the quality and quantity of the resources assigned to it are adequate. It also serves as a check on the quality of the planning itself. Any major flaws revealed at this point will require a change of plan, a change of objective, or both, as indicated by the decision branch ("no" or "yes") in the flowchart.

There are other opportunities to validate an action plan. One is the joint objective-setting discussion mentioned in Odiorne's definition. This procedure assures that the manager and the employee are jointly committed to achieving the objective. The manager commits his or her effort in helping the employee surmount obstacles and attain success. To arrive at that agreement, the manager first must be convinced of the desirability and validity of the employee's proposed objective. Two heads thus applied to the examination of the proposed objective make more than doubly certain that its conception is sound.

Results   This small single block on the flowchart represents the reason your organization exists — the production of goods or services. Lest we appear to be slighting this most important concern of every organization, we remind you that the primary purpose of everything else we are discussing is the *continual improvement of results* through better planning, direction, and feedback.

Performance review   Each employee should continually review and appraise the results, and this review and appraisal should be supplemented by periodic formal discussions between manager and employee. These activities breathe life into what otherwise might become a static and nonproductive exercise in planning. The review process consists of:

1.   The day-by-day assessment of progress
2.   The continual problem solving which keeps things moving
3.   Periodic reviews wherein the manager and the employee assess results and replan future efforts, if necessary
4.   The manager's infrequent but regular appraisal of the employee's performance and potential

The first three items are mainly concerned with the progress of the work itself, whereas the fourth is primarily employee-oriented. The first two, concerned with the day-to-day control of the work, are left in the hands of the employee, with help from the manager as needed. The periodic review and the performance appraisal, quarterly and annual respectively, are joint discussions with the manager. Performance review procedures are explained in detail in Vol. III.

Feedback   The results of the performance review and appraisal process are fed back into the ongoing objective-setting and action-planning process, and help determine changes in objectives and plans. Revision of individuals' objectives affect unit objectives as well. Feedback from the employee to the manager during the periodic review discussion may show that the employee needs the manager's help to clear obstacles from the path of progress. (Such efforts often become a part of the manager's personal objectives.) Feedback thus keeps the MBO system responsive to problems, deviations, and the need for corrective effort. The feedback does not stop at the level of the individual and the manager. Inputs from the individual level are often helpful to the strategic planning process and the reshaping of overall organizational objectives.

In the MBO process, "feedback" also means the information given to the employee about performance, in both the technical and the human relations aspects of the job. Much of this kind of feedback comes from the manager. For the employee, it fills very important psychological needs for recognition and for knowing "how I'm doing" in the eyes of the boss. It is also important that the employee have access to feedback in the form of reports or other measurement tools that give *direct* information about progress without the intervention of the manager. This kind of feedback allows the employee to exert a maximum of self-control and responsibility on the job.

Employee development　The performance review may indicate that the employee needs further training or other forms of development in order to perform the present job effectively or to prepare for future positions that may be suggested by the performance-and-potential appraisal. The MBO system may become a highly mechanistic form of management unless managers maintain and demonstrate a genuine interest in their employees' personal and professional development. This is essential to the realization of the full benefits the system offers.

We will discuss the potential benefits of both the mechanistic and the employee-centered application of MBO later in this unit, but first the series of processes leading to the individual objectives step in the Fig. 1 flowchart must be explained. These processes are essential prerequisites to the individual objective-setting process. In effect, they represent strategic planning at the "micro" level, focusing on the individual. They are analogous in many respects to the "macro" process of strategy formulation for the organization as a whole.

Individual responsibilities　Each jobholder must have a clear understanding of the reasons for the existence of the job, its key responsibilities, and the priorities each of these responsibilities carries. This may seem a truism, but it is often overlooked. The well-known example of customer service specialists who regard phone calls from customers as interruptions which prevent them from catching up on paperwork illustrates the need to get back to basics — on the part of the manager as well as the specialist!

Lacking (or losing) this perspective on the important contributions the job must provide, the employee may become embroiled in time-consuming activity that contributes little to the desired results. The employee's efforts will tend to become increasingly misdirected unless the relationship between the job and the organizational mission is kept in mind. To avoid this problem, a thorough understanding of the key results areas of the organization is essential. The KRAs are those aspects of total performance in which an organization must *continually set and achieve objectives* for improvement to preserve its health and assure its growth.

It is also important for every employee to have a model of mature, expert performance—or, more specifically, an indicator of success for each important responsibility, answering the question: "How will I know when this part of my job is being done well?" These indicators should be incorporated in the job description or other document defining the job.

Job descriptions are not a new concept. All organizations use them to list the duties of the jobholder, to give information to prospective candidates for the job, and as a guide to selection of the right individual in terms of abilities, experience, and interests. In some cases, the employee may pull his or her own job description out of the files from time to time, and refer to it as a checklist to see whether all the bases are being covered. Managers may refer to the job descriptions of their subordinates at appraisal time to refresh their memories on exactly what each person is supposed to be doing. However, the MBO process requires more than a mere list of the duties which a jobholder is expected to perform from time to time while occupying the position. The inputs from the lower right portion of Fig. 1 (leading to the individual's objectives), which provide the link between the unit or component objectives and what the individual actually contributes, come from a more sophisticated version of the job description than a mere listing of duties.

The position guide, or job description, in the MBO system specifies levels of performance for each duty or responsibility. It indicates the achievement level which a fully trained and mature incumbent would be expected to reach on the job—the ultimate in performance. Obviously, not every incumbent, especially in the first months or even years on the job, can reasonably be expected to achieve these ultimate levels of performance—certainly not if jobs are designed to provide opportunities for growth. Interim levels which *can* be achieved are therefore established to provide shorter-range targets for the new incumbent, since the "impossible dream" may not be the most appropriate motivator for the newcomer. We will describe the content and uses of an MBO job description in the final unit of this volume.

You may question the value of having two sets of targets for the individual. An analogy may be found in long-distance running. For many years, long-distance runners held the 4-minute mile as an "unachievable" but prized goal. Before that elusive record was reached, there were of course many winners along the way. Performances of long-distance runners became steadily more impressive in part because that goal existed. Along the way, however, it is probable that most runners found their real motivation in an attempt to better the fastest previous performance or to knock another second off their own best previous time.

Levels of performance　Establishing levels of performance in the form of standards of excellence — the highest achievements in the field — helps keep in view the opportunities for improvement in the routine, continuing duties of any job. In the rare case, present performance may be at such a masterful level already. Here the standard can act as a baseline for measuring deterioration in performance if it occurs. In any case, the objectives of each individual must be apportioned between the routine and the often more interesting and appealing creative projects. Having a level of ultimate performance as a reminder encourages attention to the routine.

The information system　Measurements of performance are readily established and verified in some cases, but not in others. The expense of time and effort in gathering the data necessary to assess performance against a measurement criterion that was hastily proposed can be great. The capabilities of the existing information system must be examined carefully when you prepare standards. Often information presently available will suggest a form in which the standards can be expressed without generating new data.

In any case, the climate of self-control mentioned earlier requires that the information be made available directly to the employee in a timely fashion. Ideally, the employee is the *first to become aware* of problems and has the maximum opportunity to correct them.

A STARTING POINT FOR INDIVIDUAL- IZED MBO

When this chain of prerequisite planning processes has been completed, the individual is in a position to select most effectively the objectives pertinent to the job. Once these processes are completed to the mutual satisfaction of manager and employee, the output, usually in the form of a job description of the type described above, should become a *working tool* for both, not merely a part of the permanent organization manual for the unit (which normally just gathers dust in someone's file drawer or bookcase). At the very least it should be used to prepare for the periodic performance appraisal and to guide newcomers on the job.

Preparation of such a detailed job description constitutes a method whereby you, the individual employee or manager, can institute your own test of MBO. We have designated starting point C on the flowchart as the point of entry for the individual. Though it is possible to carry out some of the essential parts of the process by yourself, the review of your performance will of course be much less subjective if you enlist the help of your immediate manager. Doing so will also give a broader perspective on organizational KRAs, unit objectives, and other inputs you will need. (It is not necessary to have formal companywide KRAs or objectives in effect. You can generate a reasonable facsimile—enough to serve this limited purpose—in dialogue with your manager.) If you are a manager, you may wish to try this same approach by selecting an employee to conduct the test of the system. If you decide to do this, don't overlook your own responsibilities in making the system work. We have referred to these responsibilities earlier, and we will discuss them at length in Vols. II and III.

FOCUS ON OBJECTIVES: REQUIRE- MENTS FOR THEIR EFFEC- TIVENESS

Selecting and writing objectives is a crucial activity in the MBO process. We stated earlier that a good objective fills three key functions: (1) to record the commitment of the writer or the organization to achievement of a needed improvement, (2) to provide a measurement of performance, and (3) to motivate the performer. Objectives can accomplish these three purposes best when they are:

written—The process of documenting what is to be done creates a feeling of commitment that a verbal agreement often fails to do. In a complex situation it also is much more reliable than memory. Conversely, beware of the person who scoffs at "writing it down" as so much red tape. This resistance may signal an unwillingness to commit oneself!

supportive—Objectives must complement the overall organizational mission. Sometimes the nature of the support is not obvious immediately—for example, the objectives of the manager of the cafeteria of a downtown bank or government agency. These secondary contributions to the effectiveness of the other operations of the bank or agency are sometimes hard to measure, and become recognized only when discontinued or poorly managed.

important—There are two things to consider here. First, the Pareto principle, stating that 80 percent of effects can be related to 20 percent of the causes. For example, 80 percent of sales volume comes from 20 percent of the customers, and—what is more specifically related to individual objective setting—80 percent of the results produced by a jobholder comes as the result of 20 percent of his or her efforts. The important objectives are those associated with maximum results. A second measure of importance is the contribution which the objective promises to one or more of the key results areas of the organization. You will recall that these are the areas in which the organization must concentrate its efforts to ensure long-term success. By definition, neglect of *any* KRA for an extended period will stand in the way of that success. Thus, if the hypothetical organization in Fig. 2 has as its KRAs cost, quality, customer service, safety, and environmental concern, every individual in it must consider objectives which impinge on one or more of these areas. The objective (probably only one of several), selected by the mechanical engineer in that organization obviously is primarily a cost-reduction project, but it can also be expected to have a favorable impact on customer service by reducing mandatory downtime on the machines.

interlocking—Your objectives must also complement the efforts of others in lateral positions in the organization. Similarly, you must recruit where needed the efforts of others in complementing your own objectives.

measurable—You must be able to find out when an objective has been achieved. This statement is often distorted to imply that every objective must be expressed in numerical fashion—quantified. *Many objectives cannot be quantified,*[2] but the requirement of *measurability* remains.

---

[2]Some MBO authorities have urged that *all* objectives be quantified, or stated in numerical terms. However, preoccupation with "the numbers" can result in the selection of relatively minor objectives that are easily stated as dollar savings, for example, to the neglect of substantial improvement needs which cannot be quantified so easily.

The measurement may be subjective, based on "feel" or judgment. In turn, feel or judgment is generally based on specific "critical incidents" which indicate that the desired objective has been achieved. An improvement in interpersonal competence of a subordinate may be measured by the absence of unpleasant confrontations with associates, for example. "Completed on schedule" is often a sufficient measurement of attainment of an objective. Such statements, however, should not deter you from seeking more precise quantification wherever possible. "Improved union relations" can be measured by frequency of grievances, proportion of grievances resolved at the verbal level, days lost by work stoppages, etc. "Increased research effectiveness" can be concluded from numbers of patent applications filed, sales resulting from products developed within the past 2 years, etc. Public relations can be measured by column-inches of favorable or unfavorable "press," by numbers of customer or citizen complaints, and so on. For most fields of endeavor commonly termed "unmeasurable," some kind of measure can be found.

results-oriented—Each objective should be selected for its *contribution* to one or more key results areas, not merely for its *activity* in that area. An objective must *have* an objective—something other than keeping the objective-setter out of mischief. On the other hand, some valid objectives *may* involve an activity which good judgment says will reasonably lead to attainment of the desired goal. For example, if the ultimate objective is to improve interpersonal relations and understanding between a city council and the administrative staff, or between registered nurses and licensed practical nurses in a hospital, an objective to complete a team-building workshop seminar between the two groups by next March is entirely acceptable. If such a meeting is competently developed and conducted by a qualified facilitator, it is a powerful contributor toward the ultimate objective of an improved intergroup working relationship. Even though this objective itself is stated purely in terms of activity and not of results, good judgment identifies it as a worthwhile and potentially productive objective. The key word here is "judgment." Both employee and manager must exercise good judgment to assure that objectives stated in terms of activity are indeed *results-oriented*.

specific and clear—These requirements are so obvious as to need little explanation. Boss and subordinate need to be able to agree at some later date on exactly what was intended. Did the reduction targeted in labor costs include indirect as well as direct labor? What base level of productivity was used in determining the 10 percent reduction—last year's budget or last year's actual? Were the desired results contingent on some specific help or action by the boss? Specificity and clarity prevent confusion over such questions. In addition, they provide greater assurance of achievability than vague, global statements of intent.

time-binding—An objective without a deadline is like a blank check. It provides the subordinate with infinite latitude and requires little commitment. Even a continuing objective toward maintaining a certain level of cost or quality for an indefinite period should include dates as checkpoints for measurement, and for review of opportunities to determine whether the targeted level is still appropriate and how it might be improved.

jointly set and accepted—Mutual development and acceptance of objectives between manager and subordinate provides the primary motivational "plus" in the successful MBO system. The principle here is that people will have a greater commitment to ideas, programs, and decisions which they have helped to create. Such commitment can be expected to result in a higher level of effort and support on the part of the subordinate. Commitment is of course no substitute for the vision and intellectual capacity necessary to *select* the best objectives in the first place, nor for the competence necessary to carry them out. But allowing opportunity for this kind of participation and commitment is a way of attracting, keeping, and providing for the continuing growth of competent people, which over a period of time can mean the difference between a good organization and a truly great one. We are speaking here not only of the initial agreement on objectives, but of the continual mutual assessment and renegotiation of objectives in a problem-solving environment. This is the type of performance appraisal we will discuss in Vol. III.

achievable—"Achievability" means two things. First, it means the difficulty of the job for the individual; it should be difficult enough to provide stretch but not so difficult that frustration is certain to result. (Recall the earlier discussion of the need for establishing two levels of performance.) Second, it means technical feasibility. As stated previously, when we set an objective we should have a plan or alternate methods in mind for achieving it. For example, an objective to improve the productivity of refuse collectors in a city organization (or maintenance mechanics in an airline terminal) by 10 percent by the end of the year is highly suspect unless one or more specific methods or courses of action can be spelled out which give a fighting chance of achieving the 10 percent improvement. When such an objective is desirable, and no feasible plan exists for it, then the formulation of a plan should be made the first-stage objective: "By December 1, evaluate alternatives for the attainment of a 10 percent reduction in indirect labor costs in the warehousing and shipping unit, and present recommended action plan to management for approval."

challenging—There is no surer way of turning MBO into a meaningless paperwork exercise than to use it simply to document what the organization is already doing. This is not only frustrating to the high performers in the organization, but it also ignores the real reasons for adopting MBO: to strive continually for improvement and to increase the responsiveness to change demanded by the environment.

supported by authority—The authority to take necessary action for achieving the objective must be delegated, not only in terms of freedom to take action, but in the assignment of concrete human, financial, and other resources needed to do the job.

backed up by a plan—The plan is an essential part of the objective itself, to verify its achievability, to identify the resources needed to accomplish it, and to provide checkpoints for measuring progress toward it. As we stated above, when no plan exists, the proper first-step objective is to develop one.

The objective-setting process is very important, since the failure of any objective to conform to these standards diminishes its value as an energizer and a directive force for the individual. No matter how thorough and sound the strategic planning, the setting of priorities, the job definition, and all the other prerequisites, the real interface between the individual and the MBO system is the short-term objective. The objective can be a clear and challenging guide to action. It can facilitate productive dialogue between boss and subordinate. It can stimulate personal growth as well as organizational accomplishment. But it can do all these things only in proportion to the care and thought put into it.

WHAT CAN THE ORGANI- ZATION EXPECT OF MBO?

MBO holds promise for an organization in proportion to the difference between its management system and the one we have described—not as its system appears on paper, but as it actually operates, and *whether or not* it is referred to as "management by objectives." There are exceptions to this rule of thumb. A military or other organization that has traditionally operated with strong direction from the top may actually be thrown off stride—at least temporarily—by the introduction of concepts such as joint objective setting and self-control. All organizations have members who thrive under strongly directive leadership. These individuals may not respond immediately to the humanistic — that is, employee-centered — aspects of MBO.

At the other end of the scale, an organization may be composed of highly creative self-starters, whose output is "discovery" and whose mode is to follow the lead suggested by the most recent experiment in designing the next one. Such people are likely to be turned off by the order, structure, and "mechanization" they see in the MBO approach.

In each of these polar extremes, however, there are potential company benefits from the judicious introduction of the humanistic elements in the first case and the mechanistic or structural improvements in the second. For most organizations the benefits of the MBO system come eventually from both sources. In fact, a management system cannot properly be called MBO unless it does involve both humanistic and structural elements.

The structural elements foster the sense of common direction, the clarity of purpose, the focus on results and standards, and the level of communication and management feedback which the audit and control functions of MBO provide. More specifically, the ultimate benefit derives from:

> Effectiveness rather than mere efficiency, "doing the right things" in addition to "doing things right"

> More efficient and purposeful communication between levels of management and between employees and their managers

> An improved mechanism for rational planning, emphasizing strengths while recognizing weaknesses, the competitive environment, and the needs of the organization's clients or "claimants"

> A more rational method for evaluating and rewarding the contributors to success, based on performance rather than on personality traits

> A generally more cohesive and informed work force, in which individuals concentrate their efforts on common goals and priorities

The humanistic elements of MBO foster employee autonomy and self-control, participation in the decision-making process, and the feedback which is clearly concerned with the individual's personal development. These are central themes of the mutual objective setting and the performance appraisal and review processes. The benefits appear in the form of a better-performing work force resulting from:

Employees' higher degree of commitment to activities, decisions, and programs which they have played a significant part in creating

Their greater trust of and cooperation with managers because of the helping attitude the latter exhibit toward them

Their realization that rewards depend not only on what gets done, but on how it is accomplished — recognizing the employees' problem-solving and coping behavior, and in general treating them as unique individuals

The interest shown in their personal growth and development

The *immediate* potential for your organization may lie in the humanistic and/or structural areas. The organization which is in disarray may well concentrate its effort first on restructuring, and may institute the humanistic emphasis at a later point. We note such an evolution especially in the performance appraisal system. The pre-MBO system is more than likely a checklist of personality traits (cooperativeness, attitude, initiative, etc.). The structural emphasis of MBO puts appraisal on much firmer ground: performance. The humanistic emphasis puts back into the equation a personality dimension, as noted above, but one which must not overlook the measures of objective performance.

To summarize, taking a polar position on the "true" meaning and purpose of MBO can result in failure to utilize its full potential. An organization may profitably introduce the system in either way, mechanistic or humanistic, depending on the present status of its management system — but always with an eye to the future benefits of going all the way.

WHAT MBO IS NOT: SOME MISCONCEPTIONS

Through the years a number of misconceptions have arisen to becloud the MBO issue. They point up the widespread superficiality of understanding to which we referred earlier. Aggravated by over-enthusiastic claims by MBO's promoters, and by the horror stories related by those who attempted to apply it without sufficient preparation, these misconceptions have created a negative climate in many organizations, preventing a rational discussion of MBO as a potential improvement in management practice. We conclude this brief overview of MBO with a list of prevalent claims and statements to which we add a few words of refutation or clarrification.

"Another new gimmick, soon forgotten . . ."

By now we hope you understand that MBO is not a gimmick, but rather a system of total management. Furthermore, it is not new. It is an articulation of management functions and processes that characterize the work of the better managers in the most effective organizations. First defined and described in the 1950s, it is not likely to die out or be forgotten as long as there is a need for creative managers dedicated to organizational improvement.

"A highly complex and theoretical concept developed in the ivory tower by academicians"

True, the concepts were first articulated in the universities, but by management authorities with a decidedly real-world orientation. These researchers and consultants made a real contribution by documenting and systematizing the very practical methods developed by their clients.

"Purports to be an 'easy out' for managers . . ."

This could not be further from the truth. MBO is a most demanding system of management. There is, as far as we know, no easy road to effective management over the long term. Some proponents have described the system as simply an informal, periodic, verbal, or "back of an envelope" contract between a manager and an employee, promising vast results. The contract is indeed a part of MBO, but the results depend on a great deal more than the contract.

"A panacea for all organization ills . . ."

Insofar as good management practices can identify and ultimately solve many problems in the organization, MBO can qualify as a "broad-spectrum" antidote. But it is no cure for incompetence, and no insurance against such forces as inflation, foreign competition, and government intervention. Its practice will build competence, but it also *requires* competence. And it can help the organization adapt to, if not foresee and avoid the impact of, the uncontrollable factors.

"A typical 'campaign': a big flurry and it's all over . . ."

Unfortunately, this is the form the implementation takes in many organizations. The initial effort is to produce a set of objectives. All levels of management set to work, the big book is published, and the whole organization lapses into a state of normalcy until the next campaign. But such an approach, as we have seen, does not produce an MBO system.

"Only for large production organizations, where output can be 'counted' "

Operations whose output can be counted tend to have an easier time of setting objectives, but they benefit most from the objectives they set in the intangible areas. Organizations large or small, whose output is all intangible — a school guidance office, for instance — need MBO even more than the production operation.

"A 'paper mill' that bogs you down in a morass of forms and reports . . ."

This is probably the most legitimate of all the critical comments on our list. Documentation *can* become a major problem. However, it can be kept under control. We will help you find the optimum in Vols. II and III.

"A punitive approach to managing people . . ."

This belief comes from early attempts to simplify performance appraisal by measuring only how fully an employee met the stated objectives. Since the employee was supposed to set the objective in the first place, MBO quickly got the reputation of "giving them enough rope to hang themselves." Needless to say, this feeling on the part of employees was something more than paranoia. It is still one of the most frequently encountered stumbling blocks in the way of implementing MBO. If these kinds of employee attitudes have been instilled by past management practices, managers must be very sensitive in handling the joint objective-setting process and in performance appraisal. At best it will take time and patience, through several cycles of appraisal and feedback, to get the point across that managers are there to help the employee be successful.

The other units of this volume deal with the strategic planning process on both an organizational and an individual level. Before turning to the next unit, however, work through the exercises for this unit. The first exercise will give you an opportunity to assess your job and your organization, as they are and as they might be affected by an MBO system of the type we have described. The second is a test of your understanding of the process.

Most of the units in this entire series are followed by one or more exercises. Try to complete each unit's exercises before reading on. You will get much more insight into the MBO process if you do the exercises.

We will offer a few words of comment or interpretation following each exercise. This is to give you feedback on your performance wherever possible. In relatively few instances do we provide answers, because the proportion of cases or problems where anyone other than you can *know* the answer is small. Most exercises (like the two in this unit) involve analysis of your own job situation or organization, or they present situations into which *you* must project *yourself.* Our commentary, therefore, is often in the form of suggestions — about facets of the problem which are typically overlooked, or about further work you can do on your own to apply the principles and methods of MBO on the job.

You will find the exercises demanding of your thought, time, and energy. Do them thoughtfully and carefully. You will get much more out of the books if you complete *every* exercise, because the exercises address important points not covered in the text. You can better understand many of the difficulties that can arise in applying MBO principles by *first* exposing yourself to the problems in the exercises and *then* reading about their possible solutions.

Finally, remember what we said in the beginning, that MBO requires a great deal of commitment. How you respond to these exercises is a test of your commitment, and probably a good predictor of your success in tackling MBO.

EXERCISE 1A   1.   List the critically important duties, responsibilities, and results which your job should, under ideal conditions, contribute to the organization.

2.   List any other duties which interfere with your fulfilling the critical obligations listed above.

3. List any problems (organizational, procedural, policy, interpersonal, etc.) which prevent you from contributing to the organization as effectively as you wish.

4. Select the most critical interferences and problems you have identified. Referring to the MBO definition and flow process diagram (Fig. 1), in which aspect or element of MBO might you expect to find an answer or solution? Describe the possible actions you might take and the results you might expect from them.

EXERCISE 1B   We haven't truly learned a concept until we can explain it to others. Listed below are several questions which have come up in introductory seminars, from managers hearing about MBO for the first time. Test your understanding of the overall process as we have presented it in Unit 1 by responding to these neophytes. Fill in the key points of your response on page 28. Practice giving the full response verbally to an associate or to a mirror.

1. "Why this laborious process of looking at major responsibilities or KRAs, thinking up 'ultimate levels of performance,' and *then* setting objectives? I know what my job is; it's to cut costs. Why not just let me set objectives — period?"

2. "It sounds like MBO just consists of writing down what I'm already doing. This is only taking my time away from doing it, and then holding my feet to the fire because I don't bat a thousand."

3. "A formal performance appraisal will do nothing but inflame my people! We don't have a merit pay system in our city. How can I motivate a person by giving her an excellent review and then not reward her with extra pay?"

4. "Suppose my manager asks my unit to contribute a share of our division's overall cost reduction target. Wouldn't I be a fool to commit myself to a figure unless I already had action plans to tell me how I'd reach that figure?"

5. "How can I be sure an employee isn't 'snowing' me with an easy objective by claiming that's all he can possibly do?"

6. "This idea of 'joint' objective setting is ridiculous. My boss passes some objectives down to me from on high, and I propose some of my own to him. What's 'joint' about that? Doesn't it just mean that I accept his, and then whatever time is left I use to work on my own?"

Statement	Key Points in Response
1.	
2.	
3.	
4.	
5.	
6.	

Commentary on Exercise 1A We suggest that you first review your entries in questions 1, 2, and 3 for clarity and specificity. If, for example, in question 3 you have tended to use one- or two-word entries such as "communication," "restrictive policy," and "uncooperative coworkers," go back and give it more thought. Identifying workable solutions is difficult if the problem is not well defined. Once the problem areas are defined, however, you should find answers to many of them in the MBO process.

You may also have been tempted to look for solutions in the MBO system that are not there. MBO is not the answer to all the problems an organization can accumulate. It will not create competent managers or technicians out of incompetent ones (though it will help identify the areas where competence is lacking). Neither will it take you out of a business you should not be in (though it may force you to answer the question of why you are in it). Keep your expectations at a reasonable level and apply MBO to systemic problems of planning, communication, control, and growth. Over time it will even help eliminate basic problems that may appear to be insoluble.

This exercise and others that focus on your own situation lend themselves to group thinking and consensus seeking as well as to individual study. The *Leader's Manual* which accompanies the series is designed to help you work with others in group sessions designed to introduce an MBO system into your organization.

Commentary on Exercise 1B Your replies to these questions might have included the following points:

1. The simple answer is that knowing where you're going helps in taking the first step. However, concentrating on the short-range objective entails two additional risks. First, by jumping too quickly to a short-term objective you may be eliminating the opportunity to do what the authorities on creativity call "divergent thinking," that is, thinking about a problem area (or key results area) broadly and thereby keeping your options open. Converging too quickly on a specific solution tends to close the gate on other, possibly better ideas, keeping them locked up in your subconscious. It also puts you in the position of coming up with a solution before you fully understand the problem. In this case,

the problem which your organization is facing may require a greater contribution from you in an area other than cost—for example, in quality or customer service. Covering all the KRAs helps ensure that your cost-oriented efforts won't hurt results in quality, safety, labor relations, or some other KRA perhaps even more important. (What *are* your KRAs?)

2. If objectives are truly just a statement of what you are already doing, you have missed the whole *objective* of managing by objectives— namely the improvement of individual and organizational effectiveness. Let's rethink your objectives. Start with KRAs and look at long-range goals. What is your job going to require of you in 5 or 10 years? You'd better start planning to get there *now.*

   If you feel that your boss is out to trap you, then your problem is more serious than your doubts about MBO—it's a problem of mistrust, and you should try to get to the bottom of it, whether or not you are operating in an MBO system.

3. Of course, you know your people better than anyone else—or do you? People *do* stay on their jobs for reasons other than pay. If your pay plan is being administered equitably, and if jobs are classified and priced so that your people can understand the structure, they should be able to accept the facts of life. (Have you *communicated* the pay plan to them?) Anyhow, it's a mistake to think that the appraisal itself is the motivator. The *real* motivation came from the opportunity to do that superior piece of work and from the achievement itself. A good performance review is merely good, positive recognition, which can help keep that motivation alive. It also affirms your interest in your employee's future growth. This interest may help *keep the employee around,* so that you'll have a good candidate when the next opportunity for a promotion or an upgrade comes along. To fail in giving positive recognition to your better performers either risks losing them from the organization entirely or encourages them to perform at the lowest common denominator. With really good employees, it's usually the former that happens.

4. This is a "chicken or egg" question. Which comes first, the objective or the plan of action? In fact, the two are inseparable, and you really can't say that you have firmly established an objective until you have examined the courses of action open to you for achieving it. The process is one of matching needs and potential contributions, and there is no guarantee that the match will be perfect the first time around. It's somewhat easier to do when you are the initiator yourself and have an innovative proposal to reduce cost, for example. In this case your cost objective becomes your own evaluation of what the results of your ef-

forts will be. But when responding to a higher-level need, it's best to give an honest estimate of what your contribution will be. If a gap exists, set an objective of identifying ways to close it.

5. At the functional level in an organization, there is no substitute for a manager's knowledge of the workers and of the technology involved in the function for which the manager is responsible. If you are new to the organization, you will of course have to rely more heavily on your technical knowledge at first. The question, however, seems to overlook the fact that MBO requires a continually dynamic management style in which manager and subordinate continue to learn about each other. The observant, energetic manager will soon spot the performer whose tendency is to hold back. MBO cannot substitute for intelligence and effort on the part of managers.

6. Some organizational needs are nonnegotiable "musts." (The corporate profit improvement target in Fig. 2 is a typical one.) Joint objective setting, however, refers to more than the fact that the objectives which an individual sets are partly "imposed" by others and partly "volunteered" by the individual. It refers also to the facts that the boss assumes responsibility for helping to remove obstacles in the way of the employee, that there is mutual agreement on the priorities of the individual's objectives, that there is agreement on personal development objectives for the employee, and that very often the boss as well as the subordinate may have to "give" a little, especially on the exact method to be used in reaching the objective. Joint objective setting also means coming to an agreement on what went wrong and what went right when the objective is reviewed, and having a mutual willingness to revise, tighten up, drop, or otherwise modify the objective based on the review.

UNIT 2

PLANNING AND THE MBO PROCESS

In the broadest terms, *planning* is defined as the process whereby we attempt to increase the probability of desired future outcomes over and above the probability of their happening by chance. At first glance, this definition appears to eliminate the need for devoting a whole volume in this series to planning, for how could any organization continue to exist if it weren't already doing a pretty good job of planning? On closer look, however, this simple definition raises some interesting questions whose answers may not be at all simple or apparent:

What future outcomes do we *want* for our organization, and why?

How do we go about selecting them?

What does the selection process consist of?

Who should be responsible for carrying it out?

What impact will a given amount of planning effort have on the probability of occurrence of our desired outcomes?

We will do our best to help you look for the answers to most of these questions. The last one may seem unanswerable. Who can forecast what external forces will arise during the period between planning and completion to dull the impact of your planning and make "chance" the overriding factor? How much planning is really justified in the face of such uncertainty? Yet these are the problems planners are paid to solve, and the good ones have developed techniques which improve the organization's chance of success. Their methods do not require precise knowledge of *whether* or *when* a certain event will happen, but concentrate instead on an analysis of *what if* it happens. What is needed, therefore, is not a crystal ball, but a thorough knowledge of the impact of the environment in which an organization operates and of the organization's capabilities for responding to it.

For the moment, however, let's concentrate on the one outcome whose probability we want you to maximize — the successful implementation of your MBO system. The activities and techniques we will discuss in this volume are a part of the MBO process itself. But at the same time they constitute the front-end work which fits our definition of planning: They help ensure success.

It is not surprising that planning constitutes a major part of the MBO system. After all, MBO is a self-supporting system of management-in-general, and management has long been defined as a series of discrete functions or activities. Those most frequently cited by management theorists are planning, organizing, directing, and controlling. We will define the planning activities in the MBO system of management as those which are highlighted in the flow diagram of the MBO process, Fig. 1 — the strategic planning process, the establishment of overall organizational objectives, the determination of individual responsibilities and standards, and the establishment of an information system to collect and disseminate the data and information needed to carry out the measurement of results. (A purist of the "activity" or "function" school of management thought might argue that dividing the total work content into packages of individual responsibilities constitutes "organizing" rather than "planning." We have no problem with that. In fact, if our terminology in any part of this series is foreign to your training or to your organization, we hope you will translate what we say into your own terms, as long as it conveys the intended meaning to all those with whom you will work.)

STRATEGY VERSUS TACTICS

We will discuss another aspect of planning later on in the MBO process in connection with the action plans supporting individual objectives. We will defer our discussion of these until Vol. II, on objective setting. Action plans are an indispensable and inseparable part of the objective-setting process, and they are best treated as a part of that activity. Such plans might be called "tactical," because they have a narrower scope and a more limited life-span than the "strategic" matters we will discuss in this volume. The difference between strategy and tactics is admittedly a rather fuzzy one, and depends heavily on one's vantage point. A long-range plan put together by an engineer, accountant, or salesperson in support of a particular career goal is legitimately considered a strategic matter for that individual, but it would be just a "detail" to the corporate executives and planning staff, and would certainly be omitted from their strategic thinking.

Nonetheless we will maintain a distinction between strategy and tactics here, as we concentrate on the broader, relatively unchanging goals and guidelines on which short-term programs and objectives are built, whether those goals are at the corporate or the individual level. At whatever level we are working, we will talk about matters strategic to that level.

We will not offer to your organization a "new" system of strategic planning, and will not even suggest that you depart from the one you are now using. As Peter Gabriel has observed,[1] what is needed is not another process for planning, but instead new ideas for the planner to put into the processes which already exist. It is certainly not a new idea that, instead of starting with organizational objectives, a company launching an MBO system should take a good hard look at what those objectives should be and why. But case after

---

[1]Peter Gabriel, "Managing Corporate Strategy to Cope with Change," *Conference Board Record,* vol. 12, no. 3, pp. 57-60, March 1975.

case in the study of MBO systems which failed, and of organizational distress in general, reveals that this is an idea which has been forgotten or has never been fully appreciated.

It is this old idea which we will develop in this book. We hope the *new* ideas will come from *you* as you examine your organizational practices, compare them with what they might become, and look for ways to make them more effective.

THE MACRO AND MICRO PLANNING PROCESSES

As noted in Unit 1, the MBO process usually is implemented at the organizational level. It is also possible, however, for an *individual* to carry it out to improve his or her job or career effectiveness — to install the process at the micro level, as opposed to the organizational or macro level. A process for establishing a personal strategic plan is prescribed in Unit 3. Here we will consider strategic planning and the roles that individuals play in contributing to the "macro" process.

Many organizations assign the work of planning and defining organizational purpose to a few top-level managers and specialists. We believe, however, that most organizations can benefit from the thinking of members at all levels — many of whom have more continuing exposure to, and appreciation of, the outside environment than do the top level. We intend to involve *you,* no matter what level you occupy in the management or professional hierarchy of your company, in the type of strategic thinking which goes on (or should go on) at the top. As the saying goes, "A good idea doesn't care who has it," and many of the better ones come from people at the middle and lower management levels.

Structuring the total work in a company so that it can be done effectively by individuals is also a part of the macroprocess. In most instances, however, individuals are called upon to help design their own jobs, establish the key responsibilities, and formulate standards. Only by understanding the job in this depth can each person participate fully and wholeheartedly in the important objective-setting and monitoring process which makes up the core of MBO.

For these reasons, then, the macroprocess of strategic planning is heavily dependent on contributions made at the individual or microprocess level. But, while microplanning is helpful to individual career planning and job design activities, from the viewpoint of the company it is rather ineffective to have many individuals working in isolation on the broader considerations of corporate strategy and goals. Some mechanism should be provided which enables them to build collectively upon each others' thoughts, consolidate their output, and transmit it to the decision makers at higher levels. (We have provided in the *Leader's Manual* accompanying this series a number of instructional and group process techniques which will help you accomplish this purpose. Those of you who will play a leadership role in installing an MBO system in your organization will benefit from studying and applying these techniques.)

RESOURCES AND THEIR ALLOCATION

The planning process accomplishes its purpose—to increase the probability of success in a venture—by guiding the decision maker in allocating scarce personal or organizational resources to the task at hand so that they provide the greatest positive impact on the results. For generations the basic textbooks have referred to resource allocation in terms of the "Four M's"—money, materials, machines, and manpower. After years of hackneyed usage this notion is again becoming a provocative way of looking at the job of management planning.

Current knowledge about the imminent depletion of natural resources such as fossil fuels, for example, changes the problem of allocating an apparently inexhaustible store of these materials into one of searching for alternate energy sources, recasting the priorities of energy uses, and even rethinking the long-accepted notion that ever-higher machine–manpower ratios can continue indefinitely to increase labor productivity by placing more energy in the hands of an individual worker. We have stated this particular problem on a global scale, but it has ramifications for industries, companies, and individuals: What is the future of our industry? Of my job? Do we foresee a discontinuity in the trend of capital intensiveness and labor productivity in our business? What is the new cutoff point in evaluating the desirability of a capital investment? Threadbare catchwords like "Four M's" suddenly seem to be triggering fresh questions which are necessary to today's and tomorrow's strategic planning process.

We will return to the strategic planning process in Unit 4. But first we will introduce another resource allocation problem, one which is already bothering some of you as you contemplate the steadily increasing demands which the management job imposes on you: the allocation of your time. Although time allocation is crucial to organizations as a whole, we will start with an individualized treatment of the time problem before going on to the organizational planning process. First, we recognize that a person to whom time is already a problem will not find it easy to accept the burden, intellectually or emotionally, of all that we are trying to convey in this series unless we first tackle the time problem. Second, the personalized planning process recommended by authorities in the field of time management is truly an application of the whole MBO process at the individual level. We feel that if you have experienced the help it can offer you as an individual you will be more prepared to try it on an organizational scale. Finally, time is a resource which does not require a conscious decision for its consumption. It passes into oblivion as quickly while we sit doing nothing as it does in the most productive use we could possibly find for it.

Since time is so difficult to capture, so limited for every person and so irreplaceable, we will assign it top-priority status and devote the next unit to *your* personal process for time management.

EXERCISE 2   Assume that you are about to leave your present position for one of greater responsibility in your organization. Consider the characteristics of a *strategy* as we have presented it in this unit:

> Related to overall purpose of company or job
>
> Having long-range implications
>
> Providing the basis for short-range plans and activities
>
> Relatively unchanging under short-term pressures and diversions (but subject to review and revision)

Also consider our definition of *planning* as the provision and allocation of needed resources. Then list below the questions you would suggest that your successor ask in formulating a strategic plan for tackling your old job:

Commentary on Exercise 2   We have forced you in this exercise to combine two concepts, *strategy* and *planning,* into one process, *strategic planning,* which we will cover in some detail later.

Your list should have included these types of questions:

What part does my job play in achieving organizational objectives? Which objectives?

Why does it exist? What would happen if it were eliminated? How can I make its continuance more valuable to the company?

What are the crucial responsibilities which the position entails?

What would I add to or subtract from the position to make it more effective?

With whom do I interact? Internally? Externally? What impact do these people have on my performance?

How should I divide my time on the job?

For whom do I really perform? How much of my direction comes from that source?

How well do the strengths that I bring to my job match what it requires of me?

What strengths do I need to develop?

To whom can I look as a model of how this job should be performed?

What measurements exist to tell me how well I am performing? What additional measurements are needed? How can I obtain them?

UNIT 3

ALLOCATING TIME
THE ORGANIZATION'S MOST PRECIOUS RESOURCE[1]

We think that we are justified in elevating time to the position of "most precious" among the resources available to an organization. The Confederate cavalry commander J. E. B. Stuart put it very simply: "Just get there fustest with the mostest." No clearer statement of military strategy has ever been made—and it holds today, for business strategy as well as military. The time element was clearly first in Stuart's thinking. Of course little would be accomplished by getting there "fustest" with nothing, but the organization which has the "mostest" today has it because prior time periods have been used wisely to develop or accumulate it.

---

[1]Much of the material in this unit has been adapted from an article appearing in the Winter 1976-77 issue of *State and Local Government Review.* Used by permission of the publisher, The Institute of Government, Athens, Ga.

Looking at the other side of the coin, business failure, we again find time in bold relief — time penalty clauses wiping out the profitability of a contract, time lost during which an eventual desperation move could have been prevented, time during which a slow inventory buildup "suddenly" became a costly cash crunch, and so on and on. The time was there to be used wisely, doled out in equal amounts to all competitors, but if we were to analyze what happened, we would probably find that it had become filled with urgent or routine tasks which crowded out what in retrospect should have had top priority. Often we would find that the amount of time needed to do a particular job had been underestimated, so that less important tasks filled the crucial period of time during which the start of that job had been delayed until it was too late.

Job experience is the best teacher of how much time to allot for the completion of any particular task, and we will not get into that aspect of time management. We will concentrate instead on techniques for increasing the fraction of your time which can be used for discretionary purposes, and techniques for making certain that this newfound time is used for the most important tasks.

By working at the individual level like this, we run the risk of encouraging you to maximize your own time usage to the detriment of others in your organization. You will find the time management literature full of "tricks" you can use to avoid being interrupted by your coworkers or to put you in control of when and how you can be contacted by telephone, and other self-centered devices to improve your own effectiveness at the expense of others who may need you. One way to avoid this is to discuss the time problem with a group of coworkers selected according to the impact which they have on each other. Several exercises to facilitate this are in the *Leader's Manual*. We hope they will help to weld a group of time-conscious individuals into a time-conscious organization in which every person's time is accorded respect.

TIME: THE DIMENSION OF CHANGE It has been said that there is no quicker way to become aware of the limitations of the human mind than to attempt to think deeply about time. To reflect on its *beginning* (or its *end*) or to try defining it quickly becomes mind-boggling. One definition, however, which is especially pertinent to the task of conducting an organization's affairs is the following: "Time is the dimension in which change takes place, just as space is the dimension in which motion takes place."[2] Since creating and managing change is the primary task of management in this hectic age, the use of time becomes an extremely important topic for consideration.

MAKING TIME: A MATTER OF MOTIVATION

Fortunately, you need not be a philosopher to use time properly, any more than you need to be an electrical engineer to conserve electricity. The only requirement to do a greatly improved job of time management is the motivation. You must *want* to improve even though you will no doubt have to change some comfortable habits, and you will have to *invest* some precious time in the beginning in order to get a return on that investment later. You won't surprise us if you ask, "How can I afford to *spend* the time to develop ways to *save* time when I'm already short of it?" We've heard that complaint many times before, even from managers who are highly skilled at spending a dollar now to save many more dollars later. Why this difference in attitudes toward an investment of time and of money? Habit is the answer. A habit is nothing more than a repeated behavior pattern which has become more rewarding to the individual than other things he or she might do instead; that is, it has become comfortable or pleasant or both. Let's face it: It *is* often comfortable and pleasant to waste time — the coffee break, the bull session, the browse through the junk mail "before I tackle the heavy stuff," the occasional daydream.

All these admittedly can be a source of renewal and refreshment for the tasks ahead. But they can be addictive, too. Indeed, the same failure can be seen in the time-waster as in the smoker who doesn't give up smoking, even though the long-range advantages are obvious, simply because it is so comfortable, so pleasant, and so satisfying to continue.

A second reason why most of us don't change our methods of using our time is the feeling that, for the most part, "These things

---

[2]F. D. Barrett, "The Management of Time," *Business Quarterly,* pp. 56-64, Spring 1969.

that cause my time to be wasted or ineffectively spent are imposed on me by others (or by the system), and are not within my control." And so, in what appears to be a very logical decision not to waste effort on attempting to control the uncontrollable, we do nothing about it. Something *can* be done, however, if we are willing to challenge the assumption that things are largely out of control.

In order to get started on the time management process, you must shake off the comfortable, pleasant habit of wasting time, and test the all-too-easy assumption that you "can't do anything about it anyhow." These first steps require considerable thought, self-analysis, and the willingness to accept the findings of that analysis. If you are not willing to make some investment of time, effort, and possible risk to your self-image, or if your time is already under control, you can *save* some time by skipping to the next unit!

THE PROCESS OF GAINING CONTROL OF TIME

A determination of *whether* there is a problem, *what kind* of a problem it is, and *how big* a problem it is constitutes the first step toward self-awareness. One way to accomplish this is to keep a time log, a record during a specified period which may be from 1 day to 1 week or longer, stating briefly how the various blocks of time were spent. Most experts on time management recommend making this analysis in 15-minute blocks, usually waiting no longer than 4 to 8 hours to do the actual recording. One might, for example, use time during the lunch hour to reconstruct what happened during the morning, and document the afternoon's activities before leaving the office in the evening.

Other authorities recommend, rather than the detailed analysis required by the time log, a short period of reflection on the activities which constitute a "typical" or "average" day (or an especially bad day), merely identifying the many *types* of activities involved and the approximate percentage of the time spent on them. This method is less burdensome than keeping a time log, and if your powers of recall are great enough, it is a quick and effective way to get started on the overall time management process. We do, however, recommend that you employ a detailed time log in refining and measuring your progress. You will find a format for doing this in the exercises at the end of this unit.

Whichever method you use, the next step is to examine the log or activity list and to analyze each unsatisfactory entry in terms of *why* you are dissatisfied with that particular use of your time, either qualitatively ("It wasn't worth my time" or "I should have been doing something else") or quantitatively ("It took me too long" or "A clerk could have done it in half the time"). Once you have pinpointed the incidents or activities causing frustration or time loss, you can categorize them in a number of different ways. You can easily predict what some of the categories will be: "Meetings," "interruptions," "reading reports," and "waiting for people" show up on many lists. You are more likely to identify the category "interruptions" from keeping a detailed time log than from an activity list. Only the detailed log is likely to reveal, for instance, that a report which should have taken no more than 30 minutes to write actually took an hour a half, because three telephone calls and two walk-in interruptions disturbed your train of thought.

The next step calls for a further analysis of the activities with which you are dissatisfied — the time wasters — according to whether you feel that the situation or the problem is one over which you have no control (externally imposed) or one in which you play an active role as villain or accessory to the crime (internally controllable). This step is crucial to success in time management. We repeat, persons who either feel that things are completely out of their control or who see no need for self-improvement are not likely to go far with an action plan.

If you have seriously and thoughtfully completed the time analysis up to this point, and if you cannot say truthfully, "*I* play a big part in this problem . . .", you are a rare individual indeed. Self-awareness is the first big step in solving the time management problem, but unless you have the motivation to complete that sentence — "and I intend to do something about it" — nothing is likely to be accomplished.

Generally speaking, a person must see that there is some kind of payoff from a change in behavior before becoming motivated to make that change. The ultimate payoff from a conscious effort to make more effective use of time may be great. We can't, of course, predict what the payoff will be for you, other than to offer the promise of increased satisfaction from accomplishing more than you thought possible — along with whatever benefits that might bring to your career and to your organization.

Sometimes analysis of the time log provides a shock which stimulates change, when we realize how poorly we are using our most precious resource. But, if you are being rewarded well by your organization in spite of your problems with time management, and if your present behavior pattern is pleasant and comfortable, those tremendous future payoffs become heavily discounted and you won't be motivated to change. Add to this the uncertainty about whether the organization will even notice if you do change — a possibility which is very unlikely if your company follows the principles and practices of MBO, but is nevertheless a concern in the minds of many people — and you have a status quo situation which will require that you make a conscious effort to move off dead center.

The prospect of "some conscious effort" is yet another de-motivator, of course, and we realize that the cards are heavily stacked against our getting you to start the change process. We will proceed nevertheless, and outline a program of exchanging old habits for new and more productive ones. We believe that the very low level of conscious effort we ask of you will produce enough early successes to make you want to sustain and improve on the program.

PROCRASTI-NATION: TIME KILLER NUMBER ONE

Procrastination is a habit common to most people, often unconsciously, and it is our first target. It is questionable whether the millions of signs adorning office walls and desk tops exhorting employees to "Do It Now!" have any real effect. But they do reflect the basic problem — namely, that most of us let lower-priority (and often more pleasant) tasks take precedence over the more important ones facing us. Because the important tasks are often fraught with personal risk, uncertainty, painful thought, and the necessity to expend large amounts of psychic energy, we tend to take the easy way out, busying ourselves with less meaningful tasks. These soothe our consciences because they do *occupy* the time and allow us to say at least that we have not been idle. Interruptions by subordinates or constituents often fill this purpose. They can be a welcome and easy out; we simply call it "the open-door policy" to make it legitimate. Since procrastination can be very insidious — it can be going on even while your time log may show a whole series of legitimate and "necessary" activities — recognizing it takes conscious and continual effort.

There is no quick way to eliminate procrastination. In trying to combat procrastination, it is helpful to keep its dangers always in mind. The external stimulus represented by the "Do It Now" sign is not as effective as the internally generated stimulus recommended by Alan Lakein,[3] which he calls "Lakein's question." This question, which you should ask yourself whenever a break between two tasks creates an opportunity for procrastination, is simply this: "What is the best possible use of my time *right now?*"[4]

The answer to the question must of course be instantly available if this is to be a useful device. This will not be the case unless you know exactly what your priorities are, since obviously the *best* use of a person's time "right now" must depend on what is *most important* to accomplish. To go further with the change process, we will describe a procedure for determining and keeping in front of you at all times the really important tasks and activities, and will explain how to make that procedure a habit.

PRIORITY SETTING The very idea of setting priorities presents problems for many people, especially those whose positions require them to respond to the needs and demands of others. The natural reaction is for a person in such a job to sit back and simply accept the inevitability of what Webber[5] calls "the tyranny of time" and to scoff at the idea of priority setting. "*Everything* I have to do is 'top priority'!" is a typical response, and one which may be close to the truth, at least in the eyes of an aggrieved customer or constituent. However, consider the old adage, "You can't do everything at once, but you can do *something* at once." Clearly, determining what thing is to be done "at once" means setting priorities, even unconsciously or intuitively. Doing this involves considerations such as which of these complaining customers has the most vexing complaint, who represents the largest group of taxpayers, or who has the most organizational clout.

---

[3] Alan Lakein, *How to Get Control of Your Time and Your Life* (New York: Signet Books, 1973).

[4] If you have an old "Do It Now" sign that you don't want to get rid of, you can rephrase the question: "What is the 'It' in 'Do It Now'?"

[5] Ross A. Webber, *Time and Management* (New York: Van Nostrand Reinhold, 1972).

This intuition is a part of the "feel" that only you can develop about your job.

DISCRE-TIONARY TIME

Not all things are emergencies or crises. No matter how urgently a job demands that the worker be responsive or "ready to serve," a certain amount of time on every job is available to be used with conscious discretion. Just as economists speak of so-called discretionary income — money left over after all current needs and obligations are met, which plays a large part in the growth of the economy — so we may speak of the efficient use of *discretionary time* as leading the way to improved time-effectiveness of the individual, on or off the job. And faced with the decision of how best to use your own discretionary time, that is, how to answer Lakein's question, you must have predetermined what the next most important job is. In short, there is no way to avoid the task of setting priorities!

Before we continue with the priority-setting procedure, we should first face up to another obstacle which may have arisen in your mind, best expressed by the question, "*What* discretionary time?" It is hard for many people to realize that there is *any such thing* in their work lives. The problem is that what little discretionary time a person has is often fragmented into such short, isolated bits that they can go by unnoticed and unutilized.

If you are so swamped with demands that you just can't seem to get the project at hand off the ground, it may first be necessary to *create* some discretionary time in order to get started on your time analysis. Sources of discretionary time (for example, the time now spent in "waiting" or "interruptions") will begin to reveal themselves as a result of your initial analysis. When it becomes available, as your time conservation program gains momentum, you will need to consolidate it into larger blocks which will enable you to make significant progress on some of those projects and programs that have been sitting on the shelf for so long because there has been no time to tackle them. (But remember that even the smallest fragment of discretionary time — the lull between bursts of activity — is an opportunity for procrastination to reassert itself. So keep on asking that vital question: "What is the best possible use of my time *right now*?")

The following suggestions may help you to find useful segments of time for planning, job improvements, and self-development:

1. Use the first 10 minutes of the day for analyzing what needs to be done, and draw up your orders for the day. (We will shortly tell you how to use those 10 minutes most effectively.)
2. Though it may be difficult to achieve, try to reserve the first hour of the day for thinking, with no telephone calls or visitors. (As we warned earlier in this unit, avoid isolating yourself from the rest of your organization selfishly or unilaterally. A much better approach is to develop a mutually accepted respect, organization-wide, for this period of ''thinking time.'')
3. Come to the office 30 minutes early in order to work without interruption. If possible, work at home half a day per week.
4. Set aside specific days in the week for meetings, problem sessions, etc. Use the remaining days for consistent continuing effort on major issues.[6]

A more unorthodox approach to gaining discretionary time for creative work involves the use of what might be called ''positive procrastination.'' This is deliberate, conscious procrastination-*with-a-purpose*—not the habitual and unproductive procrastination we warned about earlier—and it recognizes that delays may be productive under one or more of several conditions: (1) the time is not right for you to work on a certain task, because of a conflict with your biorhythms,[7] (2) you are the type of person who profits from delaying the start of a project to the point at which the deadline *demands* that it be done efficiently and expeditiously, (3) the task is of doubtful importance and might best be postponed, pending information which may indicate that it need not be done at all.

It is important to remember that any of these conditions can become a crutch and result in the development of bad habits. However, it is always useful to examine yourself (in the first two instances mentioned) and the source and credibility of the importance of the

---

[6]Taken from R. J. Craig and W. C. Turner's ''The Problem of the Manager's Time—Why Is There Never Enough of It?'' *Industrial Management,* vol. 16, no. 12, pp. 3-6, December 1974.

[7]Biorhythms are said to account for the well-known fact that some people perform at their peak in the morning and some in the evening. Positive procrastination suggests that you defer an important task until your next peak period, if you are left any discretion in the matter.

task itself (in the third instance). Much time can be gained as a result of knowing when and under how much pressure you work best, and applying judgment in the evaluating of assigned tasks rather than reacting instinctively to please the boss.

The setting of priorities may be accomplished very effectively by a combination of self-analysis and job analysis in a procedure recommended by Lakein.[8] This takes an initial investment of time—the more thought you put into this process, the better—but after a base point is established, as little as 10 minutes per week can result in keeping "the best use of my time right now" constantly uppermost in your mind, and can help you to make the best use of your time.

The steps involved in the priority-setting process are as follows:

1. Answer the question: "How do I want to spend the rest of my career?" List long-range objectives you want to reach, and activities you want to complete.

2. Answer the question: "What do I most need or want to do in the next 5 to 10 years in *support* of those long-range career objectives?" Again, list the appropriate activities and intermediate objectives.

3. Answer the question: "What do I need to accomplish in the next 3 to 12 months which will contribute the most to my organization (and incidentally, to my career objectives)?"

4. Review steps 1 to 3 as a whole, and add any activities or goals which your first answers may have overlooked.

5. Select the one objective from each of steps 1, 2, and 3 which you most desire to achieve or complete as of this moment, and write each objective on a separate piece of paper.

6. Under each of the three objectives in step 5 list as many things as you can think of that you could do *in the next 7 days* to further that objective. Do not evaluate feasibility at this point. Merely "brainstorm" as many ideas as you can.

7. After your lists in step 6 are complete, go back and scratch out any items that you do not reasonably think you can accomplish, or that you do not seriously intend to pursue. (This is the time to evaluate feasibility.)

8. From the items that remain, select the *one* item from each list that you *will do* in the next 7 days. Keep these three items in front of you at all times as the best uses for your discretionary time.

---

[8]Lakein, op. cit.

The process outlined above deserves some explanation. The purpose behind it is to awaken the realization that a permanent "drift" can set in on our careers, in which state we may be completely under the control of outside demands, and in which we are not likely to do anything constructive with our precious discretionary time. The best way to avoid this drift is to think, as in steps 1 to 3, about what we really want and what is most important to us over the long-range. Each calculated short-range action thus becomes an important step in achieving these objectives. The exercise forces us to balance our efforts between the long-range and short-range objectives, and the 7-day constraint forces us to look at what we should do "right now" in whatever discretionary time becomes available. The brainstorming feature encourages the consideration of alternatives which might not otherwise come to mind. The entire process, after the initial formulation, can be completed in 10 minutes. This makes the process adaptable to a daily rather than a weekly cycle. In fact, it is quite likely that the top-priority tasks from step 8 will be completed in less than a week, and that a continued revision of step 8 may be necessary, using the list of tasks which will contribute most to your "permanent" long-range objectives, or to other more immediate temporary targets which will inevitably arise.

We recommend that you keep such a list, with priorities categorized roughly—high, medium, or low—to provide a backlog of tasks. Review them frequently to make sure that newly added targets don't completely obscure your career objectives, although in fact they will often assume greater importance for the short term. On the other hand, your life goals are not likely to change with great frequency, and your weekly or daily review will usually start with step 4.

While lifetime planning is implied in the process, it is of course adaptable to a shorter cycle. In the term of office for a legislator, for example, the midrange objectives might cover a 1- or 2-year span.

TIME-SAVING TECHNIQUES A minimum amount of discretionary time devoted to this whole process—from time-log analysis through the eight-step priority adjustment—will almost certainly produce *more* discretionary time and greater personal effectiveness. One of the most fruitful applications of the eight-step priority-setting exercise is to use it in the early stages to set objectives and identify priority projects for the saving of time itself. For example, you might develop a system for screening incoming phone calls and making callbacks at the most effective time, or develop guidelines which will make the conduct of staff meetings more effective. An especially fertile field to explore is the more efficient handling of routine matters, complaints, inquiries, and crises. This can generate large amounts of discretionary time for more creative use. Your time-log analysis can be used to identify the needs which are most crucial to your own effectiveness.

Don't reinvent the wheel, however. There is a wide range of measures already available in the literature which can help you make better use of meeting time and tackle other time wasters such as paperwork, interruptions, and telephone time.[9] It is important to recognize that such things are necessary to any job, and that some of them may be the highest-priority tasks you have. Overdone, however, they can easily become a form of tyranny. You may need to take firm measures to free yourself from slavery to the telephone, to the unannounced visitor with a problem, or to the report which, although of questionable value, must get out on time. We must recognize the basic right to privacy in the interests of getting one's job done. Continued, unrestricted availability of managers to their

---

[9]For an extensive treatment of time-saving techniques, see R. Alec MacKenzie, *The Time Trap* (New York: AMACOM, 1972); Webber, op. cit.; and Peter Drucker, *The Effective Executive* (New York: Harper & Row, 1967).

Drawing by C. Barsotti;
© 1977 The New Yorker
Magazine, Inc.

"All right, put me on hold. I'll use the time to conceptualize."

coworkers and subordinates or to the impersonal demands of the system is the certain road to complete personal disorganization. Even the most insistent claimant on a manager's time must realize that effective management depends on an appropriate mixture of planning and responding, and must be made to understand why the manager is unavailable during certain hours. However, it is also important to let people know you can be relied upon, for example, to return telephone calls during certain specified periods. A good secretary is a vital asset in this regard, and you will find suggestions in the literature we have cited which will help the secretary to perform properly.

We have concentrated on the planning aspects of time allocation (objectives, priorities, etc.) to the neglect of specific time-saving techniques and methods. There are two reasons for this emphasis. First, the real key to time effectiveness is not how much time we can cut out of meetings, phone calls, interruptions, and the like, but *what we do* with the time we save.

Second, you may have detected in Lakein's priority-setting procedure the striking similarity to what we have described as the major steps in the MBO process itself. What you will go through in the eight-step exercise is, in fact, *MBO on a microscale.* You can verify that for yourself by matching the eight steps to the corresponding steps in the MBO macroprocess.

Like MBO, however, the benefits of this time management process lie not in understanding and accepting its principles but in the continuing application and refinement of it, and in the challenge and "stretch" which it provides to you or to the organization. If, for example, the eight-step process produces at the end a set of objectives for the week which you already knew you were going to achieve, the time management process has contributed nothing to your development other than an additional paperwork burden. Neither will MBO under similar circumstances provide benefits to the organization.

Remember that the ultimate objective of learning to manage your time is to become able to react instinctively to the passage of time. Eventually you should be able to discard all these time management tools — paperwork, time logs, catch phrases, and other artificial devices — and simply *know* what you have to do next to keep functioning at your most effective level. Some people do a very good job of this already, just as some organizations have evolved their own "MBO system" and would have little to gain from formalizing it. If you are in that category, just continue doing what you have been doing. The danger lies in assuming you already manage your time well if you really do not. We recommend the self-analytical tools we have provided here as a way of testing that assumption.

In Unit 4 we will return to the macroprocess of strategic planning, looking at that process as answering three basic questions:

1. "Why are we here?" In searching for the answer to this question, we look at the individuals and groups who have claims or legitimate demands on our organization.

2. "Who are we?" This question helps us to develop a self-image of organizational strengths and weaknesses, and an awareness of what our claimants see in us.

3. "Where are we going?" Here we use the answers to the first two questions (often expressed as a statement of organizational mission) to determine appropriate strategy and long-range objectives.

EXERCISE 3   1. Using the format shown in Fig. 3, maintain a time log for 3 consecutive days. Calculate an effectiveness rating as shown. Average your effectiveness for the 3 days and use it as a baseline measurement.
Repeat this analysis at monthly intervals as you proceed with your personal time-effectiveness program. Take an effectiveness reading each time you use the log, to track your progress.
Use the results of your initial analysis as instructed below.

2. Go through the Lakein eight-step priority-setting exercise as we have described it, in terms of career objectives and work activities. Using the results of your time-log analysis, concentrate in step 3 on objectives related to improved time-effectiveness.

Step 1   How do I want to spend the rest of my career?

Step 2   What do I most need or want to do in the next 5 to 10 years in support of those long-range career objectives?

Time period	Activity	Ratings			Comments and suggestions for improvement
		A	B	C	
8:00					
8:30					
9:00					
1:00					
1:30					
2:00					
2:30					

Rating codes (See Note 1)

    Column A: 1 = planned   2 = unplanned
    Column B: 3 = urgent   4 = important   5 = unimportant   6 = routine   7 = imposed
    Column C: 8 = satisfied 9 = dissatisfied

Effectiveness Rating for the day (See Note 2)

    A = percent of time rated "1" in Column A _____
    B = percent of time rated "4" in Column B _____
    C = percent of time rated "8" in Column C _____

$$\frac{A + B + C}{300} = \text{Effectiveness rating} \qquad _____$$

NOTES ON USE OF THE TIME LOG

Note 1:   Give every activity a rating in all three columns. Column A provides a measure of *control* of your time. Column B provides a *usage* measure. Column C is a subjective measure of your *satisfaction* with the way your time was spent.

           Column B may contain more than one digit. For instance, you may rate this morning's 10:00 meeting with the boss as a 357—urgent, unimportant, and imposed. Likewise, an activity may be a 34, urgent and important, or a 35, urgent but unimportant.

Note 2:   The Effectiveness Rating (ER) is a combined score on control, usage, and satisfaction. Each rating, A, B, and C may vary from zero to one hundred. The formula for ER obviously weights these three factors equally. You may adjust these weights as you see fit, depending on the nature of your problem. For example, if your job is composed of unplanned activities or emergencies—typical of a fire fighter or trouble-shooter—there is little point in downgrading your ER just because "That's the job." In such a case, your formula for ER might be $\frac{B + C}{200}$.

FIGURE 3
Daily time log and
effectiveness rating.

    Whatever formula you choose, *stay with it* so as to preserve a uniform basis for measuring changes in effectiveness.

Step 3 What do I need to accomplish in the next 3 to 12 months which will contribute the most to my organization (and incidentally, contribute to my career objectives)?

Step 4 Go back and add afterthoughts.

Step 5a   Write your *top* career objective from step 1 here:

Step 6a   List the actions you can take in the next 7 days in support of that objective.

Step 5b   Write your *top* midrange objective from step 2 here:

Step 6b   List the actions you can take in the next 7 days in support of that objective:

Step 5c   Write your *top* short-range objective from step 3 here:

Step 6c   List the actions you can take in the next 7 days in support of that objective:

Step 7   Go back and eliminate from steps 6a, 6b, and 6c those things which you will *not* do in the next 7 days.

Step 8   List the three top-priority activities, one each from steps 6a, 6b, and 6c, which you intend to complete or undertake in the coming week:

6a

6b

6c

Note: It is not realistic to suppose that the top three tasks in any week will always neatly distribute themselves in the manner specified in this exercise. In any given week, select all three tasks from the same category if your judgment so dictates. Over an extended period, however, it is advisable to "force" a fairly uniform distribution so that none of your objectives will be neglected.

3.   Repeat the eight-step exercise, this time concentrating on nonwork objectives. In steps 1 and 2, simply substitute the word "life" for "career." For step 3, substitute the following:

Step 3   Answer the question, "If I had 6 months to live, how would I spend my time?" (This modification forces you to look at the personal values in the answers to steps 1 and 2, and at needed actions which are easily lost sight of in the delusion of immortality which most mortals hold. Your attempt to answer this question may reveal a need, for example, to put family activities into a higher priority, or to make a will, or to schedule a thorough physical examination for yourself.)

Save the results of Exercise 3 for future use in conjunction with the exercises in Units 7 and 8.

Commentary on Exercise 3

1. Effectiveness ratings can approach 100 or can be very low, depending upon the nature of your job, your skill in managing your workday, and your degree of satisfaction with the way you are spending or investing your time. The requirements your job places on you for responding to imposed demands and for routine work are also large factors. If you are *totally* on demand or on call, for example, rating A will be 0. If, furthermore, you are *totally* dissatisfied with this state of affairs or with the routine nature of your work, rating C will also be 0. Under these conditions, your maximum possible effectiveness rating will be approximately 33 out of 100, and then only if you rate all your activities as important activities. The low effectiveness rating in this case reflects personal dissatisfaction with the job, *not* poor use of time. In any case, the real value of this exercise lies not in a single measurement, but in tracking the *trend* of effectiveness as you apply the principles of personal time management. We predict that as you find the *planned* activities increasing and the *imposed* and *routine*, or *unimportant*, activities decreasing, your satisfaction will increase. The result will be a steady increase in your time-log effectiveness rating. More important, your *real* effectiveness in the eyes of your organization will increase also.

2. It is not unusual for persons exposed to this exercise for the first time to spend most of the time simply staring at the paper wondering where to start. If this happens to you, it may help to consult with others to see what their first reaction was, or to talk it over with your manager. In any case, we hope that you will repeat the exercise at least several times before you make a final determination of its value to you. Its real value, like that of your time log, may not be apparent after the first trial.

3. Try this "nonwork" version of the eight-step process if you strike out in attempting to apply the process to the work environment. Your real time problem may be in your life away from the job.

UNIT 4

THE STRATEGIC PLANNING PROCESS

THREE QUESTIONS

The solution to the proper allocation of time lies in what you are ultimately trying to accomplish. Just so, the organizational planning process in general — which determines how much effort and resources to allocate to what activities — depends on the company's long-range objectives. These, however, are *not* the starting point in the strategic planning process.

Implicit in the selection of your lifetime or career objectives in Unit 3 were the answers to two questions of a very searching nature: "Who am I?" and "Why am I here?" Most people answer these two questions unconsciously or intuitively while formulating answers to a third question: "Where am I going?" You expressed the answers to the third question as your career objectives. We can't tell whether you actively considered or accurately answered the first two in coming up with your answers to the third,[1] but we can definitely say that an organization which bypasses this conscious self-analysis is in danger of losing its way. Yet there are many organizations which do not pay attention to these vital questions, at least overtly, and which appear to "start with objectives." In fact, it is a common criticism of MBO by professional planners[2] that the MBO approach itself encourages the objectives-first approach. Sometimes the proponents of MBO may not have made clear how to follow the objective-setting process at the corporate level. In other instances the company may have been at fault in its haste to provide a starting point so that the whole management structure could become involved "right now" in the MBO process. Regardless of the reasons, the planning process in many companies resembles the description given by Charles Tavel of the Organization for Economic Cooperation and Development. Tavel finds it typical of the majority of European and American organizations:

> *Many firms will exhibit three-year or even five-year 'plans' which actually do not offer more than a fairly consistent extrapolation of past sales or earnings trends. Hardly worth more than a budget forecast over a three- to five-year period, they are mostly based on arbitrary objectives such as ten percent sales growth or five percent increase in profits. But they do not indicate on what basis [those] figures have been [determined] or how those objectives will be reached. Their main value is to compel operational managers to survey the overall situation, to reflect on the future, and to define targets. They also provide an estimate of what the effect of recent investments is likely to be. Finally, they serve, or at least should serve, to help justify requests for new investments and to structure the company's budget. This type of plan is a tool for the management of operations. It is certainly no substitute for . . . a corporate strategy. It does not really provide for the future.[3]*

---

[1] It might be enlightening to you to attempt to consider these first two questions and then reexamine your lifetime or career objectives in Exercise 3.

[2] See for example, W. E. Rothschild, *Putting It All Together: A Guide to Strategic Thinking* (New York: AMACOM, 1976), p. 2. (AMACOM is the publishing arm of the American Management Associations.)

[3] C. H. Tavel, *The Third Industrial Age: Strategy for Business Survival* (Homewood, Ill.: Dow Jones-Irwin, 1975), p. 232.

The process as Tavel describes it does have some usefulness. In fact, it is impossible to get along without the tactical support which such an operational plan provides to the strategic purposes of the organization. However, a series of successes in the tactical battles with the annual sales and earnings budgets does not ensure long-term success—does not really provide for the future, as Tavel puts it. Conversely, given a sound long-range strategy, an occasional tactical failure need not prevent the success of the strategic plan. It is of course a fact that in the business world one tactical failure often precipitates a change in strategy, but that is a sign of a poorly thought-out strategy in the first place (or possibly one that has been formulated as an exercise, without any real commitment other than that "every company should have one"). Such "strategies" usually consist of a series of arbitrary long-range objectives which are not based on the analysis necessary to determine whether they are achievable or even whether they are the right ones for the organization.

THE FIRST QUESTION: "WHY ARE WE HERE?"

It might seem that the first of the three questions whose answers represent the heart of strategic thinking for an organization should be "Who are we?" But if "who we are" is defined as the way you and your claimants view your strengths, capabilities, and limitations as an organization—and if you accept the major premise that the reason "why we are here" is to serve those many interest groups who have varying claims on your organization—then the answers to the question "Who are we?" will be more revealing if they flow from a definition of "why we are here," rather than vice versa. Further, this approach prevents our picture of "who we are" from becoming only an inbred analysis of what we think of ourselves and reveals instead who we are in the eyes and minds of our claimants—all those who influence whether or not we are successful over the long term.

Who are these groups of people? Are there other ways for us to consider why we exist as an organization rather than to satisfy the claims and expectations of others? Table 1 lists the groups of claimants on a business firm, as they are identified by Cleland and King. We will ask you to spend some time analyzing these later, in the context of your own situation. But the question of other reasons for existence as an organization demands at least a brief hearing for

UNIT 4

Table 1
Claimants to the Business Firm*

Claimant	General Nature of the Claim
Stockholders	Participate in distribution of profits, additional stock offerings, assets on liquidation. Vote of stock; election of board of directors. Inspection of company books, transfer of stock, and such additional rights as established in the contract with the corporation.
Creditors	Participate in legal proportion of interest payments due and return of principal from the investment. Security of pledged assets; relative priority in event of liquidation. Participate in certain management and owner prerogatives if certain conditions exist within the company (such as default of interest payments).
Employees	Economic, social, and psychological satisfaction in the place of employment. Freedom from arbitrary and capricious behavior on the part of company officials. Share in fringe benefits. Freedom to join union and participate in collective bargaining. Individual freedom in offering up their services through an employment contract. Adequate working conditions.
Customers	Service provided by product; technical data needed to use the product; suitable warranties; spare parts to support product during customer use. R&D leading to product improvement. Facilitation of consumer credit. Safety in use of product.
Suppliers	Continuing source of business. Timely consummation of trade credit obligations. Professional relationship in contracting for, purchasing, and receiving goods and services.
Governments	Taxes (income, property, etc.), fair competition, and adherence to the letter and intent of public policy dealing with the requirements of "fair and free" competition. Legal obligation for businessmen (and business organizations) to obey antitrust, EEO, pollution control, and other laws.
Unions	Recognition as the negotiating agent for the employees. Opportunity to perpetuate the union as a participant in the business organization.
Competitors	Norms established by society and the industry for competitive product. Business statesmanship on the part of contemporaries.
Local communities	Place of productive and healthful employment in the local community. Participation of company officials in community affairs. Regular employment; fair pay. Local purchase of reasonable portion of the products of the local community. Interest in and support of local government. Support of cultural and charity projects. Favorable impact on environment.
The general public	Participation in and contribution to the governmental process of society as a whole. Creative communications between governmental and business units designed for reciprocal understanding. Fair proportion of the burden of government and society. Fair price for products and advancement of the state-of-the-art in the technology which the product line offers.

*Adapted from David I. Cleland and William R. King, *Management: A Systems Approach* (New York: McGraw-Hill, 1972), p. 104.

people who might not accept without a struggle such a major role for a group of outsiders in determining the fates of their organizations. For example, what about people who maintain that they are in business to make a profit and that all other purposes are secondary?

This is a difficult position to challenge. Such authorities as economist Milton Friedman and others have implied that even social responsibility is measured in terms of profit — that profitability *is* the major social responsibility of a business, and that only by making a profit can a business exercise its many other responsibilities to society. We are not downplaying the importance of profit, an issue we will deal with in Unit 7. Rather, we are pointing out that profitability is really a business objective — an answer to "Where are we going?" — and not a statement of organizational purpose in reply to the question "Why are we here?" The difference may be subtle, but it is extremely significant. Understanding this difference can help ensure that the profit objective will be achieved and will not remain an empty wish. Such an understanding also means knowing the difference between strategic planning and the type of planning which Tavel has described.

You may already have accepted the concept of organizational purpose as the satisfaction of the claims, demands, and needs of a number of interest groups, "claimants" as Cleland and King call them, or "stakeholders" as they are termed by the General Electric Company. If not, or if "to make a profit" still sounds like the best answer to the question of why your organization exists, simply ask yourself, "What entitles us to our profit?" and "What forces allow or help us to earn our profit, or prevent us from doing so?" Your answers will surely reflect a realization that profit depends on providing goods or services to customers (consumers, distributors, manufacturers, or governments) and that the cooperation, acceptance, understanding, or benevolence of many groups besides the customers (employees, suppliers, creditors, regulatory agencies) are necessary for continuing profitability. With so many influential voices complaining that businesses and nonprofit agencies are being run by and for the primary benefit of their "hired managers," the top management of any organization cannot afford to ignore the claims and interests of the many important groups which affect the organization's future.

We do not mean to imply that the interests of hired management should not be considered in strategic planning. This is the group — at all levels from the top down — which makes the organizational plan work and which should, as we said earlier, contribute much of the thinking which goes into strategic planning. The interests of all levels *must* be served if the "owners" expect wholehearted support for the organizational mission.

Neither do we want to give you the impression that simply "considering the interests" of a number of diverse groups is any guarantee of profitability. In the first place, there are too many situations in which you cannot legally or practically exercise control or influence; over your competitors, for example. There are also many cases (most, in fact) in which the interests of the various groups conflict. Finally, there is no known method by which you can evaluate quantitatively the magnitude or even the relative importance of the interests or claims of all these diverse groups, or the magnitude of the positive or negative impact each of them has on your future profitability.

Rather, the purpose of answering the question "Why are we here?" in terms of the satisfaction of others' needs, expectations, and demands is that it provides a framework in which we can better use our judgment in making decisions which establish or change the nature of the business. We are forced to consider the probable impact of major decisions on those who control our future growth, profitability, and even survival.

SERVING CLAIMANTS IN KEY RESULTS AREAS

We mentioned the idea of the key results areas earlier. The term is Peter Drucker's. Recognizing the need for multiple objectives (rather than simply "increased profitability") for a business, he proposed a checklist of areas in which the organization must pay continual attention to results, must establish objectives, and must strive for improvement in order to assure its continued success. Any organization's KRAs must be selected so as to address the needs and demands of its claimants.

Measurements in these areas determine whether or not an organizational mission is being carried out, how well, and with what sort of trend—improvement, stability, or deterioration. Each area is "key" in the sense that if any one is consistently neglected over time, the organization cannot continue to perform its mission and carry out its responsibilities to its claimants. (You should apply this test to your own proposed list of organizational KRAs.) Drucker states that the eight KRAs for a business are:

Marketing
Innovation
Human organization
Financial resources
Productivity
Physical resources
Social responsibility
Profit requirements[4]

However, nonbusiness organizations may find other KRAs more suitable to their specific missions, and even businesses have departed from or modified this list to some degree. Some firms, for example, have felt that Drucker's "human organization" should be replaced by *two* KRAs, "manager development" and "employee attitudes," to provide more specific guidance in formulating strategy and setting objectives.

SOME NONBUSINESS KRAs

KRAs should be developed to meet the specific needs of the organization and its claimants. Here are two examples which represent the thinking of two organizations, one a local government, the city of Fairfax, a suburb of the District of Columbia, and the other a quasi-governmental entity at the national level, the Federal Reserve System.

Fairfax, one of a large number of local governments in the Capitol environs, is a member of several regional agencies, and contracts with other local government bodies for some of its services. Its KRAs are expressed as "generalized objective" areas:

Strong fiscal policy and procedures
Strong contractual relationships

---

[4]Peter F. Drucker, *Management: Tasks, Responsibilities, Practices* (New York: Harper & Row, 1973), p. 100.

Support of regional agencies

Staffing for service to citizens

Sound personnel policy

Capital facilities

Public service facilities

Innovation in programs

The Federal Reserve System sets "continuing System goals" in four areas:

" *MONETARY POLICY*   *Maintain a monetary policy that accords with the principles of the Employment Act of 1946, namely, to promote sustainable economic growth and foster high employment and stable prices, with due regard for the maximum efficiency of financial markets and the free flow of funds therein, for the maintenance of orderly financial conditions, and for supporting the position of the United States in international trade and finance.*

SUPERVISORY AND REGULATORY POLICY   *Promote a sound, efficient and progressive financial system by: (1) maintaining an effective program of bank and bank holding company supervision and financial regulation both at home and abroad; and (2) administering effectively the consumer affairs responsibilities assigned to the System by the Congress.*

SERVICE AND MEMBERSHIP POLICY   *Provide, efficiently and effectively, those financial services to Federal government, the public, member banks and other qualified depository institutions that are required by Federal statutes, or if discretionary, are a natural by-product of central banking activities and cannot be effectively provided by the private sector.*

MANAGERIAL POLICY   *Manage the Federal Reserve System in a manner consistent with the highest standards of public service — a manner that will achieve the effective allocation of resources, incur the lowest cost consistent with high-quality performance, maintain the financial integrity of the institution, and place appropriate emphasis on employee accountability and motivation.* **"**

These two organizations apply the terms "generalized objectives" and "continuing system goals" to their KRAs. We cannot quarrel with their terminology; it is only a small step from a KRA to the generalized objective or goal. However, we feel it important to keep the idea of the KRA as it relates to the organization's claimants. Furthermore, we recommend that you think of the term "objective" as a *commitment* which is time-binding and satisfies all the other requirements of a good objective, as we defined them in Unit 1. Both organizations, in fact, show a well-developed understanding of this point in the specific objectives they set in these broad areas.

Note also that while the Federal Reserve System has only four KRAs, rather than the generally accepted eight, several of Drucker's recommended areas — productivity, the human organization, and social responsibility — are included explicitly in the four.

Ultimately you will be using the information generated at this point to set overall organizational objectives. The following units will demonstrate how these newly developed data are used for that purpose, first as we consider the question of "who we are" and then finally as we decide "where we are going."

Many examples could be cited of how organizations have paid for their neglect of the needs, demands, and expectations of their many claimants or stakeholders, and how major decisions have been made which failed to consider the impact they would have on one or more of these interest groups. But we feel that you will learn more from analyzing your own situation in terms of your relationships with influence groups, at the organizational, functional component, and individual levels. The exercises which follow will give you an opportunity to do this. They will also begin to make you aware of the relevance of the next strategic question: "Who are we?" (or "Who am I?")

72

EXERCISE 4   1.   Referring to Table 1 for help in getting started if you need it, list the two or three groups (or individuals, as appropriate) which you regard as having the most significant impact on (a) your total organization, (b) the component of which you are the manager or a member, and (c) your own position or role in the organization. After each one, state the expectations or demands with which you (or your organization or component) are having the most difficulty. Recall that these may be internal as well as external to the organization.

Use the table on the facing page to record your responses.

Source of Influence

	Organization	Own Component	Own Job
Group 1			
Deficiencies			
Group 2			
Deficiencies			
Group 3			
Deficiencies			

2. For each of the deficiencies you have noted, decide whether it exists (a) because of a failure to execute a present policy, procedure, or plan, or (b) because of the need for a basic change or innovation in method, direction, or concentration of effort. For each instance in which a basic change is needed, suggest reallocation or acquisition of resources to overcome the deficiency.

3. In 1962 President Kennedy publicly proclaimed that the consumer has four basic rights:
   To be safe
   To be informed
   To choose
   To be heard
   Taking your customer's point of view, how does your company rate as a grantor of these rights?

4. The Circle Chemical Co. manufactures and markets a broad line of engineering plastics materials to equipment manufacturers and the automotive industry. The company has earned a major share of these markets because of a strong marketing emphasis by top management, giving it a strong reputation for service. It is known in the marketplace as the "department store" of the plastics materials industry because of the wide range of products offered.

   The new chief executive officer came up through the financial ranks, and has been given by the company directors the charge of improving the company's profitability. One of the CEO's personal objectives is to overhaul the present individual sales incentive compensation plan, in which salary is variable, based on the dollar volume of sales measured against an annual quota. The new plan would pay a salary based on the "contribution margin" (sales volume less manufacturing cost) generated by each salesperson, and is designed to get the sales force to push the more profitable products.

   You will probably not be surprised to hear that the new plan is faring badly. The idea has found very little acceptance, and feelings are running so high that the CEO has virtually given up the idea and is looking for other ways to improve the profitability of the product mix.

Granted that the CEO would probably have been forewarned of the problems and dissuaded from the planned course of action simply by bringing the matter up at a meeting of his staff, put yourself in the position of predicting the problems without the benefit of that advice. First identify the groups or individuals who will have an influence on the success of the plan, and then predict their reactions to it.

5. Having defined "why we are here," draft a brief statement of organizational mission which summarizes the reason for the existence of your organization. What is its ultimate purpose?

Commentary on Exercise 4

1. This exercise demonstrates that the first step in strategic planning — the analysis of influence groups — can be applied at the subsystem and individual levels as well as at the organizational level. You should find both internal and external influences at all three levels. The number of outside influences you encounter as an individual will depend on whether you are in an interface position between your organization and the environment. Examples of interface positions are purchasing agent, salesperson, and public relations specialist. If you are a manager, you should have your employees on your list of influences.

   In concentrating at this point on deficiencies, we are not blindly applying that principle of dubious validity known as "management by exception." Simply stated, the exception principle holds that so long as things are proceeding satisfactorily they should not receive a manager's attention. The hazards of this rule are apparent. Even though deficiencies deserve management concern, strengths do not maintain themselves without a considerable amount of management effort to nurture them. As we develop the strategic planning process further, you will see that equal time is given to maintaining, developing, and leading from organizational strengths.

2. To concentrate on the strategic planning process, we asked you first to weed out the deficiencies that are the result of failure to execute an operational plan. Not that these deficiencies are unimportant; as a matter of fact, without the ability to handle day-to-day management problems and follow a sound operational plan, your chances of successfully executing a strategy for change are severely limited. But we will bypass this problem for the moment in order to concentrate on strategic matters.

   In asking you to propose a strategy to overcome each of the deficiencies you noted, we implied that the elimination of that deficiency was a valid organizational objective. Although that may actually be the case, we have bypassed a thorough analysis of "who we are" in doing so. The identification of the weakness or deficiency is a *part* of the answer to that question, but a thorough analysis might lead to the conclusion that your organization should *not* spend its resources attempting to correct some of the deficiencies you identified. Unit 5 will explore this point in greater depth.

   You have probably noted by now that, just as an organization has multiple objectives, it must also develop multiple strategies. So you probably found yourself developing several — for product development, for customer service, for union relations, for salaried compensation, for public relations, and so on. Multiple strategies will be discussed further in later units.

3. A look at ourselves from the customer's or consumer's point of view is another way of getting at the question of "who we are." Note the implications for various strategies in the areas of product development and customer service which arise. With regard to the customer's right to choose, for example, we can see internal implications for marketing and product development — for example, giving the customer the freedom to choose among our own products — as well as the antitrust, monopoly, and concentration problems which are usually raised in connection with the issue of consumer choice.

4. The customers, of course, represent the main group of outsiders on whom this proposal would impinge, although one might certainly expect that the major competitors would soon get wind of it and take appropriate action. Internally, the sales force, the sales manager, the product planners, the product development group, and even the cost accountants would feel the effects for various reasons. For the most part, this will be evident but will evolve from the question, "Why are we here?" A typical objection might be that you can't stop a salesperson from selling, and if you don't want to sell a product you shouldn't give it to the sales force in the first place. For their part, the product planners and the development people have been doing what they think is their job: to provide the customer with a line broad enough to discourage him from dealing with the competition. And the accountants can see nothing but a rash of complaints from aggrieved salespeople about the cost allocations which make their favorite products "undesirable" under the proposed policy.

   In short, an a priori analysis of those who would have an impact on the success or failure of the plan might have led the CEO to conclude that a reengineering program for low-profit items might be a more viable strategy for profit improvement. (But then the question arises: Can we continue to be all things to all people?)

   The CEO might also have concluded that it would have been best to avoid specific details of planning and leave them to functionally competent subordinates, concentrating instead on such questions as whether a company can indeed be all things to all people. If so, the CEO is beginning to see the importance of asking, "Who am I?"

5. There are no firm rules which dictate the format, length, or style of an organizational (or personal) mission statement. The statement should, however, contain some clear indication of who you feel are your most important client groups and just what you expect to provide them in the way of products, services, satisfaction, compliance, or whatever is appropriate — in other words, your KRAs. Give yourself bonus points if your statement recognizes the need for selectivity and the problems of allocating scarce resources.

UNIT 5

THE SECOND STRATEGIC QUESTION

WHO ARE WE?

In the preceding unit we identified those persons and groups upon whom your job and your organization have an impact, and who in turn have needs which you are in business to fill, or whose demands and expectations shape your actions. Defining those needs, demands, and expectations helps us answer the first of our three basic questions: "Why are we here?"

THE SECOND QUESTION: "WHO ARE WE?" In this unit we will help you think about the second strategic question: "Who are we?" First you will be asked to define "who you are," with the help of the insights gained from your own analysis of your job or your organization in terms of the strengths and weaknesses it brings to the claimants or influence groups. These insights, in turn, will help define the present or future role you see for yourself or your organization. Too much self-analysis or introspection can result in loss of touch with reality. You will therefore need to obtain confirmation of your own analysis from the claimants themselves, wherever it is possible and economical to do so. This "reality check" will reduce the danger of false assumptions or incomplete data leading to invalid conclusions about yourself and your role.

THE THIRD QUESTION: "WHERE ARE WE GOING?"

Units 5, 6, and 7 will complete the strategic trilogy. They will address the question you have been awaiting: "Where are we going?" To answer this one, you must set long-term or strategic objectives, organizational or personal. You select these objectives to lead from your major strengths and capabilities, and to overcome critical deficiencies. A major side issue we will confront in this connection is the problem of the moving target which your rapidly changing environment presents to you and your organization, and which makes in-depth long-range planning seem like a waste of time to many managers.

THE ROLE OF ASSUMPTIONS IN STRATEGIC PLANNING

The first step in the planning process is to formulate a set of assumptions about the future, about the plans and intentions of the competitors, and about any other aspect of your environment over which you have no control or about which you have less than perfect information. The impact which these assumptions can have on the validity of a strategic plan is easy to see: "The inflation rate will not exceed 5 percent per year over the next 5 years." "There will be no major competitor entering the market during the period covered by plan." "The OPEC nations will be forced to reduce crude oil prices by 10 percent by 19__ and will engage in no further curtailment or embargo measures." "Consumer disposable income will continue to increase at a rate equal to the average of the past 5 years." A significant error in any one of these assumptions is obviously enough to send the planners back to the drawing board as soon as the error becomes apparent and, more significantly, to turn any major investment of resources made up to that point into a waste or a liability rather than an asset.

We will deal with these types of assumptions in the next unit. For now, however, we are more concerned with those which arise in your own assessment of who you are. Persons and even organizations form assumptions about themselves, based on what has happened to them in the past or on what they have seen happen to others. These tend to lead to a prediction of nothing more than a continuation of past trends or, in other words, to an assumption that the same thing will happen inevitably if you expose yourself to the same situation again. The result is that people lay themselves open to errors in self-assessment. The errors may be in either direction — assuming strengths that really do not exist or overlooking real or latent strengths: "Direct mail promotion is not our bag. We've tried it several times with no results." Or "If Consolidated can do it we can. Let's give it a whirl." Or "I'm just not a public speaker. The very thought ties me up in knots."

Of course, we can't advise you on whether your assumptions about yourself or your organization are valid. However, we propose three analytical procedures which we urge you to use in your self-assessment and which will help you reach that decision for yourself. We will state them now, and give you the opportunity to apply them in the exercises at the end of this unit.

1.   In assessing a strength or a weakness, ask whether there is hard evidence that it exists or whether and to what degree an assumption has been made. Then if the evidence is not concrete, current, and credible, ask what *contrary* evidence exists. Look searchingly and deliberately for contrary evidence, because the *confirming* evidence, weak though it may be, can always be found. After all, it is the very basis for the assumption in the beginning.

2.   Examine the confirming evidence, asking yourself in each case about the source. If it is hearsay or otherwise indirectly reported, inquire into the credibility and motives of the source. If it is an inference based upon what has happened to others, ask yourself what factors or variables might be different in your case as compared with the other person or organization. If the evidence is an experience which you have had personally, ask what conditions might prevail *now* which did not exist *then* and which might have a different influence on the outcome today.

3.   When all the evidence is in, weigh the confirming evidence against the contrary evidence to arrive at a judgmental rating of the validity of your assumption. In many cases this analysis may be unnecessary because

the strength or the weakness may be quite evident. A simple test question will help to determine whether the analysis is needed: "If this assumption were false, would it lead to a course of action which would significantly detract from progress toward our goal?" If the answer is yes, accepting the "obvious" assumption without question would be unwise.

There are other types of assumptions which particularly affect our assessment of personal strengths and weaknesses.[1] Consider, for example, the statement we quoted earlier: "I'm just not a public speaker. The very thought ties me up in knots." The first assumption is that there is a negative association between success as a public speaker and the syndrome of being "tied up in knots" beforehand.

---

[1] We are using the words "strengths" and "weaknesses," in spite of their possible negative connotations, instead of the more popular euphemisms "assets" and "liabilities." In the first place, we are assuming that you (and your organization) are mature enough to call a weakness a weakness without suffering severe psychic damage. Second, the use of "assets" and "liabilities" connotes quantifiable, precisely measured entities, which most personal and organizational strengths and weaknesses definitely are not!

"Of course you have strengths, dear. It's just that you don't communicate them."

As most public speakers know, that "weakness" is found in the *best* speakers, and in fact may be a necessary condition for a performer to do his or her best. The second assumption in this statement implies that the weakness, if it indeed were one, is basic, uncorrectible, and final. Some weaknesses are practically in that category; that is, a large investment in corrective effort would produce little change. But others, as in this case, are simply the result of lack of skill, experience, or exposure, which might be obtained at a much lower cost. This of course is something the strategist must ascertain in determining "who we are."

MEASURING ORGANIZA- TIONAL STRENGTHS AND WEAKNESSES

All meaningful measurements of humans and their organizations involve comparisons with others. Even if you know a person's height to the nearest sixteenth of an inch, you cannot describe that person as "tall" or "short" except in comparison with the surrounding population. In measuring organizational strengths and weaknesses, we will use three standards for comparison. The first is what claimants or influence groups demand, expect, or need from you or your organization. The second is to what extent your competitors are meeting those same needs, expectations, and demands. (This second comparison group may be your peers or organizational components doing similar work, if you are conducting the analysis on the individual or intraorganizational level.) The third yardstick measures strengths against the needs of your own organization. The results of those three separate analyses combine to give the answer to the second basic question, "Who are we?"

AREAS OF ORGANIZA- TIONAL STRENGTH

Before these three comparisons can be made, it is necessary to develop a generalized listing of the types of resources which characterize your type of organization—city government, hospital, business, or whatever it may be—and then to take inventory of where you stand today (taking into account whatever trends or plans you already have well under way which would make a "snapshot" view of the quantity or quality of today's resources inappropriate for looking into the future). This generalized list should be in terms which allow comparisons with your competitors. For example, Rothschild recommends[2] that resources be identified in the following categories, which are generally applicable to most organizations providing products or services: (1) conception/design, (2) production, (3) marketing, (4) finance, and (5) management.

Although nonbusiness organizations can also benefit from considering their products in light of functional areas, there are some alternatives. For an institution of higher education, one might consider using the following as functional areas for internal analysis and external comparison: (1) instruction, (2) research, (3) public service, (4) support services, (5) funding, (6) placement and student services, and (7) administration. If you are in a local government organization, you might select: (1) cultural enrichment, (2) social services, (3) public works, (4) revenue sources, (5) fiscal controls, (6) public information, (7) public safety, (8) planning, and (9) management.

Within each of these functional areas, services, or "product lines," the specific breakdown of resources will be a product of your own deliberations. What makes sense to you is what counts. The only requirement is that you keep your KRAs and the needs of your claimants in mind. A typical list, conforming to the functional breakdown we have enumerated for a business organization, is shown in Table 2. However, before you attempt to list and analyze your own organizational resources, we will give you two more ways to look at your organization. These, along with the functional breakdown, may help you to avoid overlooking vital needs.

The first of these considers the organization as a series of subsystems having as their common role the survival and growth of the firm in the face of a hostile environment or internal forces which might disrupt it. These are described by Katz and Kahn as: (1) transformation or production, (2) maintenance of structure, (3) boundary maintenance, (4) adaptive, and (5) managerial.[3] The purposes, motivating forces, dynamics, and some of the mechanisms and manifestations of the workings of these systems are shown in Table 3. For a more detailed treatment of this systems approach, which

---

[2]W. E. Rothschild, *Putting It All Together: A Guide to Strategic Thinking* (New York: AMACOM, 1976), Chap. 6.

[3]Daniel Katz and Robert L. Kahn, *The Social Psychology of Organizations* (New York: Wiley, 1966), Chap. 4.

considers an organization analogous to a living organism, we refer you to Katz and Kahn. The utility which it may have for you in the present context of resource analysis lies in the possible identification of resource capabilities and requirements which might not come to light by the more conventional analysis of Table 2. For example, an analysis of your adaptive subsystem might identify the need for a competitive intelligence activity in the marketing or management

Table 2
Resources and Capabilities Characteristic of the Major Functions of a Business

Conception/ Design	Production	Marketing	Finance	Management

Human resources
  Basic research
  Development
  Paraprofessional
  support
  Consultants
	Human resources
	  Operations
	    Supervision
	    Operatives
	  Support staff
	    Quality control
	    Materials
	    Engineering
	    Maintenance
	    etc.
		Human resources
		  Sales force
		  Headquarters
		
		Product planning
		system
		
		Forecasting
		system
		
		Market position
			Human resources
			  Auditing
			  Cost accounting
			  etc.
			
			Cash management
			
			Bank relationships
			
			Credit and collec-
			tions policy
				Human resources
				  Succession plan
				  Depth of talent
				  Development
				    Philosophy
				  Sources
				    External
				    Internal
				
				Planning system

Facilities
  Library
  Laboratory
  Model shop
  Analytical support				

	Facilities and plant
	  Automation
	  Age
	  Economic size
		Customer base
		  Diversification
		  Size mix
		  Growth prospects
			Investment
			analysis
			
			Capital budgeting
			system
				Objectives
				
				Values
				
				Entrepreneurship

Copyrights				
Patents	Inventory systems	Advertising	Control reports	Information system

Design concepts	Warehousing
	  Location
	  Response
		Distribution chain
		  Dealers
		  Distributors
		  Manufacturers'
		  representatives
			Debt structure
			  Leverage
			  Marketability
			  Earnings coverage
				Control systems
				
				Organization
				  Decentralization
				  Adaptiveness
				  Decision making

Organization				
Incentives to creativity	Computerization			

Liaison linkages
  Foundations
  Universities
  Government
  DOD
	Process capability
	
	Safety and plant
	protection
		Service policy
		
		Warrantees
			Computerization
			
			Etc.
				Motivational
				system

	Cost control	Application engineering		Union relations
Etc.	Customer orientation Etc.	Etc.		Innovation Etc.

Table 3
Formal Subsystems of Organizations: Their Functions, Dynamics, and Mechanisms

Subsystem Structure	Purpose	Motivation	Mechanisms
Production: primary processes	Task accomplishment: energy transformation within organization	Proficiency	Division of labor: setting up of job specification and standards
Maintenance of working structure	Mediating between task demands and human needs to keep structure in operation	Maintenance of steady state	Formalization of activities into standard legitimized procedures: setting up of system rewards; socialization of new members
Boundary systems Production-supportive: procurement of materials and manpower and product disposal	Transactional exchanges at system boundaries	Specifically focused manipulation of organizational environment	Acquiring control of sources of supply; creation of image
Institutional subsystem*	Obtaining social support and legitimation	Societal manipulation and integration	Contributing to community; influencing other social structure
Adaptive	Intelligence, R&D, planning	Pressure for change	Making recommendations for change to management
Managerial	Resolving conflicts between hierarchical levels	Control	Use of sanctions of authority
	Coordinating and directing functional substructures	Compromise solutions vs. integrative (innovative, synergistic) solutions	Setting up machinery to adjudicate internal conflicts.
	Coordinating external requirements and organizational resources and needs	Long-term survival; optimization; better use of resources; development of increased capabilities	Increasing volume of business; adding functions; controlling environment through absorbing it or changing it; restructuring organization.

*That which maintains contact with government and public influence groups.

Adapted from: Daniel Katz and Robert L. Kahn, *The Social Psychology of Organizations,* (New York: Wiley & Sons, Inc. 1966). Copyright Wiley & Sons, Inc. Used by permission.

function. A closer look at the boundary systems might highlight a need or a capability in the college recruiting activity or a need for development of alternative sources of raw materials. We suggest that you use some of this type of analysis to augment the lists in Table 2 by doing the exercises at the end of this unit.

A third and final vantage point from which to view your organization comes from the organizational effectiveness model depicted in Fig. 4. This considers the three basic contributions to organizational effectiveness (OE) as falling into three categories — relating to its people, its technology, and the structure which provides direction and control.

The contributions in the *people* category consist of the attitudes, skills, experience, interpersonal competence, supervisory

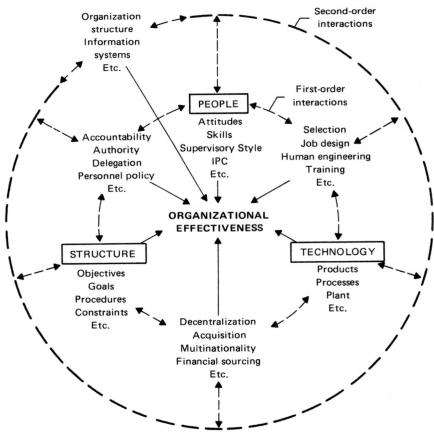

FIGURE 4
The effectiveness model of an organization: Resources viewed as augmenting the human, technological, and structural dimensions of effectiveness and interactions between them.

SOURCE: "Whatever Happened to 'OD'?" *Industrial Management*, vol. 18, no. 1, pp. 9–12, Jan.-Feb. 1976. Copyright The Industrial Management Society. Used by permission.

styles, and all other strengths and weaknesses which characterize the human resources of the firm.

The *structure* in which the people carry out their activities is not organizational structure in the usual sense, but is composed of the objectives, goals, procedures, policies, and controls which give purpose, direction, and internal constraint and discipline to the organization.

Technology consists, of course, of the products, processes, facilities, tools, design concepts, patents, and functional know-how which are used by the members to carry out the purposes of the organization.

As Fig. 4 shows, the multitude of activities which make up the fabric of organizational life are viewed in this model as interactions between two or among all three of the basic dimensions of effectiveness. Any activity has an influence on organizational effectiveness not only directly but through its facilitating or inhibiting effects on the people, the structure, and the technology. This model therefore provides an independent method for assessing an activity for strength or weakness. The method consists of analyzing the activity in terms of the force it exerts on the three basic contributors to effectiveness—or conversely, in terms of the requirements which each of these places on the activity itself. For example, is the degree of authority given to subordinates consonant with the needs and capabilities of the people involved and with the structural requirements of company objectives and controls? Is a proposed acquisition or satellite plant likely to augment or conflict with present structure and technology? Are jobs in the factory, office, or field location presently designed so that the people interact as effectively as possible with the technology they must administer or exploit? Finally, what demands do all three primary contributors—people, technology, and structure—place on the organizational structure, the management information system, or other complex activities (the second-order interactions in Fig. 3)?

The three contributors to effectiveness are very broad and general in nature. The model is primarily useful, therefore, in providing one more criterion for determining the effectiveness, or strengths and weaknesses, of activities and subsystems such as those identified in Tables 2 and 3, embodying the product or functional approach and the systems approach.

STANDARDS FOR ASSESS-MENT OF ORGANIZA-TIONAL STRENGTHS AND WEAKNESSES

At this point, we have arrived at three different bases for comparison, which you may combine or use separately to provide as exhaustive an analysis of your organization as circumstances require. First, how does each activity measure up against the needs, desires, and expectations of your claimants or stakeholders? Second, how do your activities contribute to the various subsystems of Table 3 in relation to the purposes which they must fulfill? And, finally, what effects do the activities have on the basic dimensions of organizational effectiveness—people, structure, technology? The models thus fill two needs: they serve as a basis for identifying critical activities, and they provide a series of external and internal standards against which to measure the effectiveness of those activities.

ANALYZING THE COMPETITIVE ENVIRON-MENT

In making a full assessment of the identity of your organization and its position in the market, you must also compare the organization with its competitors. (While at first glance it might seem inappropriate for a government organization to make such a comparison, those of you who are in that field will find it useful in deciding whether to provide a service internally or to purchase it from an outside source—refuse disposal, for example. Likewise, many costly investments can be avoided or postponed by "regionalizing" the most efficient facility—a water treatment plant, for example—among a group of closely situated and, unfortunately, competitive jurisdictions.) In determining the strengths and weaknesses of competitors, extensive work at the overall organizational level with the systems or organizational effectiveness models is not normally possible. These models cannot be employed by an outsider who does not have the necessary knowledge of the inner workings of the organization. This problem does not exist to as great an extent when your analysis is at the component or individual level within your own company. For the most part, however, you will find Rothschild's functional model most helpful. The sources of information which you may use to conduct this analysis within legal and ethical bounds include competitors' annual reports; the call reports of your own field sales force; the annual rankings, news items, and articles appearing in *Business*

Week, Forbes, Fortune, the *Wall Street Journal,* and other business periodicals; and information provided to members by numerous trade and professional associations.

You can obtain much useful information on your relative standing with your competitors by conducting a mail or telephone survey of your customers, clients, or other claimant groups, who have information of the type you are seeking. The requested information will of course avoid probing into any areas where the request would intrude on the confidentiality of supplier-customer relationships. While this puts limits on the amount of "hard" data which you can obtain by survey methods, the survey is especially valuable as a reality check, as we indicated earlier, to confirm the assumptions which you have made of your own strengths and weaknesses.

PULLING IT ALL TOGETHER

Figure 5 summarizes the process we are pursuing in this and the following two units. You can now identify today's organizational strengths and weaknesses as the presence or absence of a gap between what exists and what is needed. Again, as in Unit 4, you will have to wrestle with this rather demanding process in the context of your own organization, component, or job. In the preceding section we considered explicitly only one aspect of the environment: competition. But the social, economic, political, and technological aspects of today's environment have been included implicitly in your analysis, through the various claimants, who in a real sense make up today's environment. In Unit 6 we will explain how you can analyze your organization's environment, not as it exists today but as it is likely to change in the future, so that your long-range objectives, strategies, and plans will be consonant with or adjustable to future needs as best you are able to predict them.

LEADING FROM YOUR ORGANIZATIONAL STRENGTHS

At this point, however, you are equipped to make a preliminary analysis of the unique capabilities and strengths of your organization, as compared with those of your major competitors, and of its comparative weaknesses. This analysis will provide you with guidelines for the most effective allocation of your time and other resources, leading from strengths and avoiding (or making plans to eliminate) areas of present weakness. Wise strategists will refuse to do battle except on their own terms.

This is a difficult prescription for many organizations to swallow. The personal values of one or more top managers may have a major influence on what an organization strives to become. Often such an influence is powerful enough to outweigh the most thorough and

FIGURE 5
Who are we? and
Where are we going?

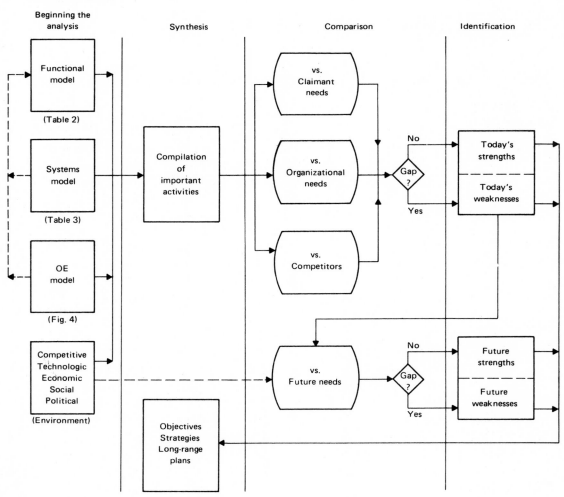

rational analysis. If you are faced with this kind of negative reaction to your strategic planning efforts, you may feel that the die is already cast and the analysis will be just so much waste motion. However, as a demonstration to yourself and to others in your company of the value of your analysis, you may wish to try it first on one component of the organization—perhaps a major project or a new product development group.

At the same time, the personal values of top management may be entirely rational and unshakable, regardless of your efforts to demonstrate what the organization might become. The owner who values craftsmanship and intends to sell only to those who feel like-wise and are willing to pay for it is not likely to consider using the skills and strengths of the company to enter the mass market, even though the required resources are readily accessible and the prob-ability of great rewards is high. In this kind of situation, the disappointed strategist would do well to consider the advisability of either leaving the firm or confining the strategy to the more limited alternatives which make sense to top management. (Of course, a strategist who had ambitions to enter the mass market and who had done a thorough job on the *personal* strategic planning process would not have chosen such a firm in the first place. We will come back to personal strategy in Units 8 and 9.)

A complete analysis of the type we propose is obviously a major effort—not within the capability of a single person, nor one to be completed in a very short time. The exercises which follow are there-fore highly selective and designed only to demonstrate the principles. Wherever possible, you should enlist the cooperation of a colleague and work together, either on the same aspect or on com-plementary aspects of your organization. The dialogue which develops during the process is essential to its most effective use.

In Unit 6 we will begin to address the third basic question of strategic planning—"Where are we going?"—by considering trends in the environment within which you and your organization are operating. Emphasis will be on forecasting the nature and impor-tance of these trends, because an important corollary to this question is: "Where is the environment—social, political, technolog-ical, and economic—trying to take us?"

EXERCISE 5   1.   Using column headings (suggested by the functional model in Table 2) which are appropriate for your organization, list the activities and capabilities which you feel should be included in the assessment of strengths and weaknesses. Use the systems and OE models to supplement the functional analysis.

2. Refer to your results from Exercise 4. Using the same two or three claimant groups you selected in that exercise, pick the one or two activities from part 1 of Exercise 5 which are most important in meeting the needs of each of your claimant groups. Analyze each activity for attributes which fully meet the needs of the group and for those which fail to do so. Decide whether the activity should be listed as a *strength* (all significant needs are met) or a *weakness* (a significant performance gap exists).

Claimant group	Activity 1	Positives	Negatives	Strength or weakness?	Activity 2	Positives	Negatives	Strength or weakness?

3. Make a preliminary analysis of your own organization and your chief competitor on the matrix below. List in the four quadrants (or "cells") the areas in which (a) you both have strengths, (b) you are strong and the competitor is weak, etc.

Your Own Organization

	Strengths	Weaknesses
Strengths		
Competitor		
Weaknesses		

Commentary on Exercise 5

While they provide an opportunity for you to practice the thought processes and logic involved, the exercises in this brief volume can only hint at the scope and depth of thought required to do a complete and thorough job of strategic planning for your organization. Furthermore, the results may be misleading when the analysis is done out of context with the rest of your organization and its claimant groups who were not included in your selection. A capability which may appear as an outstanding strength in the limited analysis you have done up to this point may actually appear as a weakness in the final reckoning, particularly in cases where there are conflicting claims by outside groups not included in your analysis, or where the needs are in transition and may be quite different 5 years from now.

Here are several examples of problems involving such conflicting claims and changing needs, which may help you to rethink your analyses in Exercise 5, number 2:

1. A union relations policy which has been highly successful in producing low wage settlements, but which is in obvious conflict with the needs of the union membership and becomes a weakness in dealing with employees. (The General Electric Company's former policy known as "Boulware-ism" is a case in point.)[4]

2. An outstanding capability for automated mass production of simple metal shapes in high volume at a time when customers' needs are shifting to small-volume specialty shapes.

3. A highly developed fund-raising capability based on public concern about a type of childhood disease for which a vaccine has been introduced experimentally with great success.

4. A unique ethical drug product with dramatic antibiotic properties but with side effects which regulatory authorities are concerned about.

---

[4]Named after that company's Vice President for Employee Relations at the time, the policy of Boulware-ism was based on one, and only one, thoroughly researched contract offer which responded as fully as possible to the employees' needs and wants. This "full and fair" stance avoided the "Eastern bazaar" bargaining process which, in the company's view, often resulted in the Union striking to get the extra concessions they felt management was withholding. This policy was deemphasized after a long strike-free period when it became apparent that it was no longer fully responsive to membership needs. Furthermore, at least in the Union view, the policy was thwarting Union leadership needs for the maintenance of power and the continuity of the Union itself.

Exercise 5, number 3, uses a deliberately rough competitive analysis in order to illustrate a technique of use in determining your organization's competitive stance. The capabilities in which your own organization and the competition rate "strong" are those which are to be maintained or perhaps given less emphasis in the future, depending on the attractiveness of other opportunities. Such opportunities are often found in the opposite cell, where you both rate "weak." (On the other hand, the areas of weakness may merely reflect a general lack of need.) The strategy of the firm should exploit the capabilities in which your organization shows strength and the competitor is weak. The remaining cell contains indications for strategies designed to avoid confrontation in areas where competitive strengths can be met only with weakness. Of course, if the opportunity is sufficiently attractive, a catch-up strategy may be indicated, using new resources or using resources diverted from the "strength-strength" quadrant.

In practice, you would of course do a much more painstaking job of rating your competitors, using whatever intelligence sources are available to "score" the key activities on the functional model of Table 2.

In a multiproduct, multimarket enterprise, a separate analysis of this type should be made for each product line or each market area, whichever is more appropriate. This more detailed analysis should reveal opportunities for greater selectivity and concentration within product or market areas.

UNIT 6

ASSESSING ENVIRONMENTAL TRENDS

The third basic question is: "Where are we going?" At this point in our guided tour through the strategic planning process, we have provided you with the tools for answering in depth the first two questions—"Why are we here?" and "Who are we?"—in terms of organizational strengths and weaknesses with respect to (1) the needs and demands of your client groups and (2) your competitors. You are now in a position to draft a much more precise and useful organizational mission statement than the one which you proposed earlier (see Exercise 4, number 5). You will be even better prepared to do so after reading this unit. The reason for waiting is that the assessment of the changing environment may throw a new light on your answers to the first two questions as they will be viewed 5, 10, or 25 years in the future. While your *current* strengths and weaknesses dictate a major portion of your short-range (1- to 5-year) strategy and objectives, an as yet undetermined portion of total resources must be devoted to assuring that you acquire or develop the strengths which the next generation of clients and competitors will require of you.

COPING WITH CHANGE

It has become a cliché to state that we live in an era of rapid change. Nevertheless any organization which is making strategic decisions whose results will not be felt until sometime in the future but which require major commitment of resources *now* must take rapid change seriously. Today's decisions must be made with the best possible forecast of what rapid change means to your organization.

The difficulty of forecasting economic, social, political, and technological change has forced many organizations into a variety of responses. Many give up the strategic approach and simply drift with (or spend a large amount of effort *fighting*) the changes which have already made themselves apparent. Others simply make linear extrapolations of present conditions. When the economy is booming, the sky is the limit for such firms; when the business climate turns sour, they lead the pack in retrenchment measures. This of course is the stuff of which economic recessions are made, as businessmen lie low and postpone or forego investment decisions in favor of tightening ship. Such moves do often provide a sounder basis on which to build — inefficiencies are eliminated, productivity is improved, sick or inappropriate businesses and product lines are phased out, and other changes are made which will provide benefits to the firm relatively independent of whatever social, technological, and political changes are in store. (We say "*relatively* independent" because such changes by individual firms may combine to increase measurably the rate of change in the environment. For example, a high rate of "technological" job losses may trigger more and more governmental action to cope with a persistently high unemployment rate.)

Other organizations, when faced with unpredictable change, closely monitor changes in areas which affect the firm's interests, and take action only when the true nature, direction, and magnitude of the change become clear. This approach has been called "innovative imitation."[1] Although it may seem to be a rather casual and weak approach to planning, the strategy of staying loose and keeping one's options open may be the most viable of all. At the individual level in particular, this strategy may be especially appropriate at the career-development stage, when one's lifetime objectives may be furthered equally by responding to different types of opportunities for lateral moves or promotions.

A more complex response to change has been brought on by questions about the future of change itself. Studies such as *The Limits to Growth,*[2] the real concerns of the ability of Spaceship Earth to sustain the human race if present trends in population and energy usage continue, and the obvious shift in values of much of the younger generation from materialism to simpler ways of living, all raise a serious prospect that change in the future may become regressive rather than growth-oriented. On the other hand, this makes it all the more necessary to follow the strategic approach to planning. The outstanding firms which have embraced the strategic planning process and made it a way of life at all levels in the organization realize this, and are today incorporating this type of thinking into their strategies. The best of these approaches, when examined closely, reveal a mixture of the strategic and what may appear to be tactical,[3] the expansive and the regressive. Risk taking is tempered by risk *analysis* and *control;* cash-sink new ventures are pursued by

---

[1]Theodore Levitt, "Innovative Imitation," *Harvard Business Review,* vol. 44, no. 5, pp. 63-70, September-October 1966.

[2]D. H. Meadows et al., *The Limits to Growth* (New York: Universe Books, 1972). This study of factors limiting the growth of the world system—agricultural production, natural resources, population, industrial production, and pollution—was initiated by the Club of Rome, an informal organization of international authorities in the fields of science, economics, education, health, government, and industry. Its pessimism has made it highly controversial, but it has awakened world leaders to the need, yet unfilled, for strategic planning at the global level.

[3]Many "regressive" (as opposed to "growth-oriented") moves which a firm may take—belt-tightening, cost reduction drives, plant closings, massive "outplacements" of personnel—may create the impression that they are serving only the immediate end of maintaining profitability in a current crunch. This may indeed be true in many cases, as we have pointed out earlier; however, they may equally well represent carefully planned strategic moves designed to strengthen the long-range future of the business. If they have the latter motivation and truly contribute to that future, then they deserve to be called strategy. In too many cases, however, the long-range results are merely a deterioration of capital, financial, or human resources.

turning older businesses into cash sources; energy-conserving new appliances and devices are developed and older products are phased out or redesigned for greater energy efficiency. The emphasis in these organizations is on achieving a balance. With the sudden but belated awareness that untamed growth can destroy us all, this blend of the two types of strategies is essential for all kinds of organizations to consider.

TYPES OF CHANGE

We have characterized the main features of the changing environment as economic, technological, social, and political. The purpose of this unit is *not* to make you expert in the techniques and methods of forecasting change in any of these areas. The forecasting business is a highly specialized one, and if you intend to *use* forecasts of environmental change in making important business or personal decisions, you should seek professional services. We do feel, however, that a brief treatment of each of these areas will give you an awareness of sources and methods. In addition, it will stimulate the types of questions you should be asking of yourself or your organization so that you will not overlook the impact of the changing environment on your strategic planning process.

ECONOMIC FORECASTING

Economic forecasts are certainly the most familiar, widely used, and essential of the four types we are considering. Without an economic forecast of gross national product, rate of inflation, and many other necessary indexes, forecasts of market growth, pricing, cost levels, and other variables have little credibility. While proprietary research and development information may give the individual firm a better "handle" on future market growth than linking such growth to economic indexes, the latter, in general, play a heavy role, especially when mature markets are involved.

The U.S. Departments of Commerce and Labor, the Federal Reserve System, major commercial banks, brokerage firms, business periodicals, universities, and consultants are all sources of historical indexes and forecasts for use by businesses and nonprofit organizations.

Much of the forecasting of overall economic aggregates is done by manipulation of mathematical "econometric" models, the more sophisticated of which express overall economic activity in terms of dozens of variables such as housing starts, automobile purchases, defense expenditures, exports, inventory levels, transfer payments, wage rates, farm output, and many others. Though only the largest firms and organizations might find such models useful in total, sophisticated models do represent a fertile source of ideas for the smaller organization which might wish to experiment with the development of a simplified econometric model. A limited model of this sort might contain relatively few variables but prove quite useful in predicting the trends for a product line that is only a small part of the economy as a whole but is of great importance to the individual firm. The techniques of regression analysis (the statistical manipulation of data which provides the coefficients in such models) are easily understood, and the calculations can be carried out on pocket computers of only moderate sophistication.

The input-output analysis of Harvard's Wassily Leontiev has potential for use in forecasting the effects of an acceleration or decline in the growth of one industry upon another industry which is an outlet for the first industry's goods or services. The U.S. Department of Commerce periodically makes available the most recent analyses of the inputs and outputs of the several sectors of the United States economy, with an extensive industry-by-industry breakdown of the manufacturing sector.

Economic forecasting of demand, even though it is the most highly developed of the several types with which we are concerned here, has severe limitations. Its time horizon is relatively short, since reliable projections of the variables which enter into the prediction are often not available beyond a few years into the future at most. Further, the forecasts of the variables themselves are heavily weighted by experience, or in other words, they may be no better than a linear extrapolation of what is happening right now. When many variables are involved, it is quite possible for an individual economist, who has no model or computer but does have a good "feel" for the situation, to make forecasts which on the average are as accurate as those obtained at great expense by the econometricians. (Perhaps, in retrospect, we must admit that the linear extrapolation of response to change, mentioned earlier in this unit, may in fact not be a bad way to go, provided the forecaster keeps a close watch on leading indicators which presage a change. Information on these indicators, as they apply to the economy as a whole, is available in the *Business Conditions Digest* of the Department of Commerce. From this information, you may develop indicators that could prove useful within your firm, agency, or organizational component.)

As we have pointed out from time to time in this volume, the techniques and thought processes of strategic planning are useful to the manager of a component within a firm, and even to the individual. This is true also in forecasting the future. For example, regression models or much simpler decision aids can be developed which will assist the manager of a staff component in predicting future demand for the services of the component. Models may also help individual managers to predict which industries or firms will be the best outlets for their own talents in the future. Similarly, the methods of technological and sociopolitical forecasting which follow may prove useful at whatever level in the organization you are working.

TECHNOLOG-ICAL FORECASTING

Technological forecasting involves the prediction of *what* innovations or changes may appear in a field and *when* they may be expected to occur. Since it concerns itself with what and when, rather than with "how much," technological forecasting (as well as sociopolitical forecasting, which is covered later) is usually called "*qualitative*," as opposed to "*quantitative*" (economic) forecasting. Qualitative forecasts are often accompanied by probability statements with respect to the occurrence or the timing of the event, but their use does not require further quantification. Qualitative forecasts are used primarily in predicting the nature and rough timing of technological breakthroughs and other major changes in the environment. The results lend themselves more to the development and selection of alternative strategies than to the setting of specific objectives. (We will deal further with this distinction in Unit 7.)

Probably the best sources of the technological forecasts that are of most concern to a firm are the research and development activities of the firm itself. The future impact of products, processes, and services which are already in the development stream can be estimated with some degree of confidence. However, the real purpose of technological and other qualitative forecasting lies not in estimating the effect of internal forces over which the firm has a high degree of control, but in predicting the changes in the external "uncontrollable" environment.

The main question you should be seeking to answer is: "What major technological breakthrough or development is likely to arise during the planning time frame which will necessitate revisions in present strategy?" This may be asked either at the organizational level, or by you as an individual concerned with obsolescent skills and the necessity for continuing education and personal development.

A workable technological forecast can be made and continually revised by simply keeping abreast of the technical journals in your field, searching the U.S. Patent Office abstracts,[4] monitoring the meetings or proceedings of pertinent trade or professional associations, and analyzing intelligence from the field provided by customers and other contacts. In order for a forecast of this kind to be effective, it is necessary to set up a command post or clearinghouse for the information gathered, and to assign definite responsibility for the collection, analysis, and dissemination of the material.

Longer-range forecasts of technological developments where there is little "intelligence" available on which to make predictions may be accomplished in several ways. We will confine our description to one of these: the Delphi technique. (Sources of others are given in the annotated bibliography at the end of this volume.)

The Delphi technique may be used to answer the following types of questions:

> What technical developments are most needed in the particular field (for example, to accelerate the transition to the cashless, checkless society, or to reduce home video recorders to the $150 to $200 price level, or to mechanize the harvesting of cucumbers)?
>
> Which of these developments is most critical as a bottleneck?

---

[4]It may seem contradictory to apply the term "forecast" to technology already existing and covered by patents. However, considering the time lag between patent and commercial development, as well as the uncertainty of the latter ever occurring, there is much to recommend forecasts based on the analysis of newly issued patents.

In what order are the developments likely to occur?

In what time span will the developments occur?

An alternative way of stating the major question is in terms of what is *likely* to develop, or in the case of the individual, what demands for new skills may be *forced* on the person or the profession. We should also point out that "technology" is a broad term, which covers the techniques and methods of marketing, production, distribution, health care, transportation, office administration, and many other fields. Even though technological forecasting originated in highly sophisticated think tanks such as the RAND Corporation, the techniques are widely applicable in less exotic fields.

A Delphi forecast is made as follows:

1. A panel of experts is formed by the coordinator. Each member's expertise may be limited to only a portion of the field in which the forecast is being made, but all should be familiar with the state of the art in the field as a whole. The panel may be composed entirely of members of the same firm or organization, or may represent other interested firms, consultants, and academicians. In any event, they are instructed not to discuss the problem with any other panel member until the forecast is complete.

2. The question is put—by letter or memo—to each member of the panel with instructions to list, rank, give dates, or provide whatever information is sought. They are at this point instructed not to inform each other of their answers. They then return their individual responses to the coordinator.

3. The coordinator compiles the results and gives them to each panel member, giving the ranges and variability. In the case of general disagreement, each member is asked to comment. In the case of individual deviation from a general agreement, each dissenting panel member is asked to reconsider or to justify his or her position.

4. The coordinator compiles the resubmitted results and repeats step 3. This compilation will generally show a narrower spread of predictions.

The process may go through an additional cycle of revision. After two or three times around, the output may reveal some degree of consensus, but the results must be tempered by judgment if a few of the expert panelists remain unshakable in their deviance.

At best, a Delphi forecast has questionable reliability, but it does provide some kind of road map into an otherwise uncharted future.

Some critics of the Delphi forecast regard it as nothing more than an exercise in conformity. However, the procedure does tend to give pause to the wildly optimistic panel member, in addition to some motivation to the overly conservative, as all the members become aware of the different feelings of a body of respected colleagues. Finally, assuming that each of the experts selected has a potential role in making happen whatever is being predicted, the process may be a subtle motivator through the commitment to progress which the experts have made while formulating their forecasts.

SOCIO-POLITICAL FORECASTING Delphi forecasting may be useful in assessing events and trends in the social and political environment as well as the technological. The prediction of *what* societal patterns, value changes, life-style changes, and other trends are likely to develop has already been the subject of much work by the futurologists of the Hudson Institute and other organizations devoted to that task. Business people or organizational leaders are therefore by no means "starting from scratch" and can readily find alternative scenarios of the future development of our society to use as a basis for forecasting the impact of that projected society on their own organizations or on themselves.[5]

The art or science of "futurology" is too much in its infancy to have proved itself to be of major value in forecasting. Like technological or qualitative forecasting in general, at this stage in its development it is little more than informed speculation about the continuation of present tendencies or about the probability and timing of discontinuities in those trends. Probably it can never be more. Indeed, it *need* never be more to perform the function we are asking it to fill here. It has done its work if it has helped raise questions which prompt the consideration of strategy alternatives oriented toward the needs and demands of the client groups of the

---

[5]One of the most current of these, *Conference Board Report 710* (New York: The Conference Board, 1977), is the transcript of a meeting at which industrialists, social scientists, educators, and government representatives discussed the new pressures and substantial changes in the business environment. This meeting was the end product of a year-long examination undertaken as part of the reappraisal of America's future that marked the Bicentennial celebration.

future. The organization must of course limit the amount of *risk* taken in committing itself to strategies based on such speculative, qualitative forecasts. But the *incremental* risk in adopting a strategy which considers sociopolitical trends compared with one which does not may in fact be quite small.

While weather forecasting techniques have been developed to the point at which a tremendous data base can now provide assurance that there is a 90 percent chance of showers tomorrow, all that this really means is that whenever the "weather map" in the past has looked the way it does today, nine times out of ten there have been showers on the following day. History, our "map" of past societal changes, is valued for its lessons. In many areas of political and social change, we can see events and trends developing which resemble past events. Tempting though it may be to make probability statements on the basis of these similarities, it is important to remember that these past events and trends were by and large unique to their times and their culture and can provide little basis for quantification.

No one can know the "true" probability of a future event. Instead, we use our own "subjective" probabilities. Where social or political events and trends are concerned—war, riots, legislation, unionization, arms limitation, government regulation—their subjective probabilities of occurrence are highly dynamic. Like the stock market, these probabilities vary with each rumor, accomplishment, disappointment, or change of leadership in the pertinent field.[6] Probability statements, then, may introduce more noise than information into the sociopolitical forecasting process.

It would be foolish to develop a strategy based on a single reading of the probabilities of occurrence of the significant trends or discontinuities in the organization's or individual's future. Instead, sociopolitical forecasters recommend the development of several (at least three) scenarios of the future upon which alternative strategies can be based. Strategies thus developed recognize the "what if" consequences of environmental developments with potentially high

---

[6]We must also recognize that, just as the process of measurement may change that which is being measured, the process of forecasting similarly has an effect on what is being forecast. This is particularly true when the forecaster plays a significant role, intentional or otherwise, in determining what happens. Recall the motivating effect of taking part in a Delphi forecast.

impact and face the organization with the need to make a choice. But at least the choice will be an informed one. It is to be hoped that the chosen strategy (or the one receiving the greatest allocation of resources) will contain at least some major elements which are common to the others.

GENERAL ELECTRIC'S QUALITATIVE FORE-CASTING: A PIONEERING EFFORT

A prime example of qualitative forecasting is provided by the General Electric Company, a pioneer among the larger corporations in developing and implementing methods for assessing future environmental impact on the firm. The company has integrated socio-political forecasting with the more established forms of economic and technological forecasting, using some unique tools developed for this purpose.[7]

The values profile analysis, a forecast of changing values in our society (see Fig. 6) is an important feature of the General Electric forecast, since changes in our value system may be the key determinants, indeed the very embodiment, of the social and political trends of the future. The direction and magnitude of the predicted changes in values are therefore quite useful in generating thought on the key events and trends in the various aspects of the environment.

Analysis of values is only a small part of GE's method of coping with the complexity of the total environment. For further analysis, the forecasters divided the total environment into nine facets. Panels of experts then took a separate "tunnelized" look at each facet: geopolitical and defense, international, economic, social, political, legal, technological, manpower, and financial. In each of these areas a listing of probable significant future events and trends was compiled. The integration of these relatively independent outputs was accomplished by a technique known as "cross-impact analysis," in which all possible pairings of events are examined to determine whether the probability of occurrence of each is affected by the other. This analysis revealed a small number of probable chains of events each of which was developed into a scenario of the

---

[7]These are described in Ian H. Wilson's "Socio-Political Forecasting: A New Dimension to Strategic Planning," *Michigan Business Review*, vol. 26, no. 4, pp. 15–25, July 1974.

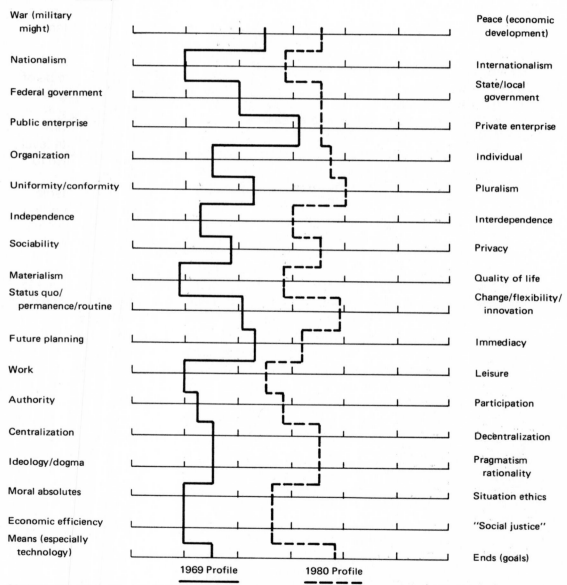

FIGURE 6
Profile of significant value-system changes: 1969–1980 (as seen by General Electric's Business Environment Section).

SOURCE: Ian H. Wilson, "Socio-Political Forecasting: A New Dimension to Strategic Planning" *Michigan Business Review,* vol. 26, no. 4, p. 24, July 1974. Used by permission.

future as seen by the company. The individual businesses within the company were then able to factor these scenarios into their own current assessments of specific capability and technology to form a sounder base for long-range strategy determination.

The rationale which GE uses to support a considerable effort in sociopolitical forecasting is that current events are eroding the roles of the traditional underpinnings of the American business system: company loyalty, "hard work," managerial authority, "private" corporate property, profit, growth, and technology. Continued erosion of these values or substitution of others must therefore be of crucial concern to the firm, and corporate planning must recognize and consider the resulting effects on strategy. There is ample evidence that GE takes its sociopolitical forecast seriously. The company recently completed a major reorganization of its corporate-level management specifically to allow the three-man executive office to devote more attention to developing sociopolitical trends.

In this unit we have completed the description of the strategic planning process depicted in Fig. 5 up to the final synthesis step, the generation of strategies and organizational objectives. Strategies will be the focus of Unit 7, and organizational objectives will be covered in Unit 8.

EXERCISE 6   1. For each of the following categories of environmental input, list the two or three major foreseeable trends or events which you feel will have the greatest impact on your organization:

Legislative or regulatory:

Technological:

Life-styles:

Demographic:

International:

Financial:

2. What major capability deficiencies and/or resource gaps do these trends (from Exercise 6, number 1) create which your organization will need to overcome?

3. Develop a mission statement for your organization which reflects (1) your assessment of the priorities of the needs of your client groups, (2) your organization's major strengths and weaknesses, and (3) the changes in self-concept imposed by foreseeable environmental trends.

4. Draw your own value-system profile for 1990 (Fig. 6). Have the predictions of the GE forecasters for 1980 been borne out?

Commentary on Exercise 6

1. Examples of general trends or events which might have found their way into your lists are:

   An embargo on imports of a critical raw material (e.g., Rhodesian chrome)

   Removal of tax exemptions on municipal bonds

   A ceiling on usage of natural gas in your plant locations

   Increasing pressures for filling managerial positions with women

   A decrease in numbers of single-family dwellings

   An aging consumer population

   Unionization of public employees

   Legislation severely limiting surface mining operations

   Repeal of Taft-Hartley section 14B

   The electronic transfer of funds

   Decreasing family size

   Acquisition of a major competitor by a firm which will complement its strengths

   A Communist takeover in an important international market area

   Increasing education level of the work force

   The spread of western European-style industrial democracy

   The breakup of major oil or auto companies

   (We are certain that your list also includes a number of items more specific to your organization.)

2. In many cases the events you have listed (and/or which we have listed above) would require major changes in the operation of your business; in other cases, even though they have a high probability of occurrence, they can safely be omitted from further consideration. It will help to categorize each item on the combined list (yours and ours) by quadrant in a matrix like the one below. The "high-impact" items should all be considered as you proceed with strategy formation.

Probability of Occurrence

	High	**Low**
Impact on Organization — **High**		
Low		

3. Since making your first intuitive draft of a mission statement (Exercise 4, number 5), you have done a great deal of thinking about served clients, key results areas, organizational strengths, weaknesses, future capability gaps, environmental discontinuities, and—a factor not to be ignored or forgotten—the values of top management (which may be your own). As noted earlier, the length, writing style, and form of the mission statement may vary widely from writer to writer, but the content is important. Check your statement for clarity in expressing or reflecting the following:

What you bring to your customers or clients

Recognition of your key results areas

Selectivity to stress strengths in service or product areas

Statement of standards of product or service reflecting your strengths

Recognition of rights and demands of other claimants

Recognition of need for change in capability

Commitment to change in capability

The mission statement is an enduring declaration of purpose and should not include specific objectives or other shorter-term milestones which would require frequent modification (e.g., not ". . . will establish seven additional Eastern suburban branches by 19__," but ". . . will maintain existing standards of service and accessibility to served-area population as projected market growth and distribution continues").

As we noted in Unit 4, some organizations consider the mission statement to be an expression of their "continuing objectives," a set of relatively permanent guidelines for the establishment of strategy and the setting of specific, time-binding objectives. Considered in this way, the "continuing objectives" function for the organization in the same way ultimate standards of performance (see Unit 1) function for the individual.

Compare this statement with your original mission statement from Exercise 4, number 5. You should notice a significant improvement in clarity and utility as a starting point for strategy formulation.

UNIT 7

STRATEGY SELECTION

In Unit 1 we defined the essential characteristics of a strategy as: (1) its relationship to overall purpose, (2) its long-range implications, (3) its basis for short-range plans and activities, and (4) its relative stability and constancy of direction when placed under short-range pressure. The analysis in Units 4 to 6 has added the use of present and future strengths and weaknesses as a fifth essential. At this point your organization should be able to select those strategies which will provide best for the future and which will make best use of your present, developed, and acquired resources. The development of strategy to meet these criteria will naturally result in more closely focused, meaningful, and realistic organizational objectives.

Critics of MBO have cited as a failure inherent in the system the presumed requirement that the organization must start with overall long-range objectives or goals. Although we have discussed this misconception of MBO earlier, it is worthwhile to consider again the viewpoint of Rothschild[1] that strategic planning converts an objective from merely a hopeful statement of what is *desirable* into a reasoned commitment to what is *possible* making the best use of all resources. This strategic approach obviously involves the optimum deployment of the organization's resources, existing, strengthened, or acquired, in the places where they are likely to be most successful in carrying out the organizational mission.

A sound strategic position is a mode or posture of resource deployment which will allow an organization to be most effective in its key results areas. It recognizes that no organization can be "all things to all people," that the resource base must be focused in the areas of greatest product or service opportunity, and that leading from or building on strengths is generally more productive than competing in areas of weakness. Many attractive objectives compete for the scarce resources of the organization. If *all* these objectives are sought indiscriminately and without selectivity, it may not be possible to achieve *any* of them.

It therefore makes sense to think about strategy alternatives and their selection before discussing objective setting, although the more accepted procedure is to set objectives and then formulate "strategy" to achieve them. We feel that this is incorrect usage of the term "strategy," and prefer to use the much more straightforward and unambiguous term "action plan" in this context. (Volume II deals at length with the critical relationship between objectives and plans.)

Either way you look at it, of course, you are confronted with a chicken-or-egg question. In fact, it is necessary to consider both objectives and strategy alternately, adjusting each until you obtain a reasonable fit between what is desirable and what is possible.[2]

As a point of departure, however, and as a guide for strategy selection, you have the organizational mission statement you developed in Unit 4 and revised in Unit 6. Such a mission statement

---

[1]W. E. Rothschild, *Putting It All Together: A Guide to Strategic Thinking* (New York: AMACOM, 1976).

[2]It may happen that this process results in objectives which are unsatisfactory in terms of the mission statement or in terms of the demands of one or more of the various client groups. This is the point at which to ask some searching questions: Should we take a new look at our mission? Are the resources devoted to this business (or this share of our business) *contributing* to the business or merely suboptimizing performance elsewhere? (In other words, are we "spread too thin"?) Such issues will be covered in Unit 8.

does not meet the rather stringent requirements of a clear, precise, measurable objective statement (which we will discuss in detail in Vol. II). But it does serve as a concise statement of purpose and self-concept (the latter confirmed by the "reality checks" of Unit 5) against which strategies and organizational objectives can be measured for their consistency and contribution.

CLASSIFICATION OF STRATEGIES

There are as many different types of strategies as there are sub-components appearing on the organization chart of the most complex business, government, or social organization. Indeed, as we have mentioned repeatedly, every *individual* in an organization has or should have a job, career, or life strategy. (Every reader who seriously and fully uses this series of texts *will* develop such a strategy.) Considering the great diversity of specific needs for strategy development among our readers' organizations, it would be impractical to attempt to cover even a small number of the fields represented. We will therefore confine this discussion to a simple classification of strategy needs and sources which will be useful as a checklist when you tackle the job of articulating and selecting specific strategies to reflect your own technologies and needs.

Product Strategy

Of first and obvious importance is the strategy which ensures the delivery of the right goods or services to your primary client group, the direct recipients of your output. Depending on the type of organization, you may think of them in other terms, but they are your *customers,* whether they are clients, consumers, equipment manufacturers, depositors, borrowers, parishioners, citizen tax-payers, patients, policy owners, tenants, addicts, students, or needy families. We will refer to this primary posture as "product strategy."

You must consider the possibility that you need a separate and distinct strategy for each segment of your product array (or each type of service you perform), and for each discretely different market in which you operate. You may ultimately decide that a single strategy will fit more than one product or market, but this should be a thoughtfully considered conclusion, not one arrived at by default.

We will return later to a model for product strategy development to guide your thinking.

Functional Support Strategies

Supporting the enterprise as a whole or facilitating the execution of the primary product or service strategies are those which develop, maintain, and allocate the many resources in the functional areas of the organization. For a business firm, the functional elements of design, production, marketing, finance, and management, as shown in Table 2, represent a starting point for consideration of support strategies. Unit 5 contains suggestions for appropriate functional classifications in other types of organizations.

Some functional strategies support specific products or services and are thus very closely related to, or even considered a part of, the product strategy itself. Others are applicable across the board, in support of the whole organization. An example of the latter is the combination of finance and personnel strategies expressed in the following statement:

" *A continuing survey and periodic upgrading of the salary plan and the employee benefit package will be made, and adequate funds allocated, to maintain total compensation at the highest level in the industry, so that the company may attract and retain top-quality employees in the professional, technical, and skilled trades categories.* "

OTHER TOOLS FOR STRATEGY FORMULA- TION

To help you assess the need for articulating specific strategies, refer to Table 3, the rather unconventional representation of the operating functions or subsystems necessary to assure the survival and growth of an organizational system. In Unit 5 you used this analysis to some extent in determining your strengths and weaknesses. Since you derived your primary product or service strategies from this analysis, it is quite appropriate to take another look at how best to utilize these subsystems in support of those strategies. If you did not use this type of analysis before, it may be even more revealing to you now.

There is yet another viewpoint from which to examine needs for specific strategy articulation and formulation—in terms of the key results areas where basic measurements of organizational effectiveness are made. Every KRA you judge to be important to your organization must be closely examined to ensure that product or functional strategies are formulated to address the needs in that area. In so doing, you will assure allocation of resources that will allow the organization to satisfy present and future claims and demands in all the KRAs. Without these allocations, improvement needs in areas critical to survival may be impossible to achieve.

**THE PERVA-
SIVENESS OF
MARKETING
AND PROFIT-
ABILITY**

There is some obvious repetition in the foregoing exposition of strategy sources and needs. In particular, we find "marketing" involved when considering product strategy, as a functional supporting strategy and in looking at subsystem performance. We find it again listed among the key results areas. This repetition, rather than being redundant, merely reflects the primacy and the pervasiveness of the needs and demands of the primary claimant of any organization: the customer. The analysis we have suggested will not permit the strategist to forget that important fact.

Managers often refer to their strategies for growth, acquisition, international business development, etc., as if these were ends in themselves. We prefer to think of such things as alternatives available for carrying out the primary product or marketing strategy. This view focuses our attention on the mission itself rather than on the means chosen for accomplishing it. Too often, the preoccupation with growth, acquisition, and multinational status has diverted companies from their primary mission. When growth becomes an end in itself, trouble is in store. International Harvester and Westinghouse are two of the better-known examples of firms that have recently recognized this problem and have undergone painful readjustments.

Profit, in contrast to marketing, did not appear specifically in our analysis until we articulated it as a KRA; however, it is equally pervasive, of course. For the business firm every type of strategy we have considered is "profit strategy" as well. It often enters the picture as its alter ego *cost,* which over time has come to include social cost in addition to the elements of product cost as they have long been calculated.

Even in government or other nonprofit organizations, "profit" is still a major consideration. Regardless of the fact that the right-hand side of the equation *Revenue − Cost = X* is zero for some organizations and (ideally) positive for others, when *X* is *negative* both are in trouble. This kind of trouble is not always evident or immediate in government as long as borrowing remains a feasible option. An equally insidious problem exists when a governmental unit carelessly (or even, as is sometimes alleged, deliberately) increases its costs to equal its revenue. Such action in effect represents a formal profit strategy, but one without a clear purpose other than ensuring against any decrease in the flow of life-sustaining revenue. In any case, it is clear that even though the term "profit" may seem inappropriate, the relationship between revenue and cost *must* be a major concern of the manager in a government or other nonprofit organization, and this concern should pervade all strategic thinking.

A MODEL FOR STRATEGY FORMULA-TION

To help you get started on the difficult and complex job of formulating a strategy for your company, agency, or component, we will describe a generalized process you may use with minor variations. This process can be a guide in formulating either product strategy or functional supporting strategy. We will deal first with product strategy.

The development of product or service strategy starts with your definition of the product and service strengths and weaknesses, as determined in the analysis of Unit 5. Include weaknesses in your strategy formulation when they represent opportunities or are critical to the organization's future, but not when they would allow vitally needed resources to be used merely to "back losers." Figure 7 shows this process and the subsequent steps. We first form a 2x2x2 cube, or three-dimensional matrix, and enter our products or services into the cells, according to whether we have high or low market position and whether we foresee high or low market growth. "Market position" in this figure refers not only to the *percentage* of the market held by the product but to the *strength* the firm shows in the marketplace. The "growth" dimension of the matrix refers not only to growth in *volume,* but to growth in *importance* and *general attrac-*

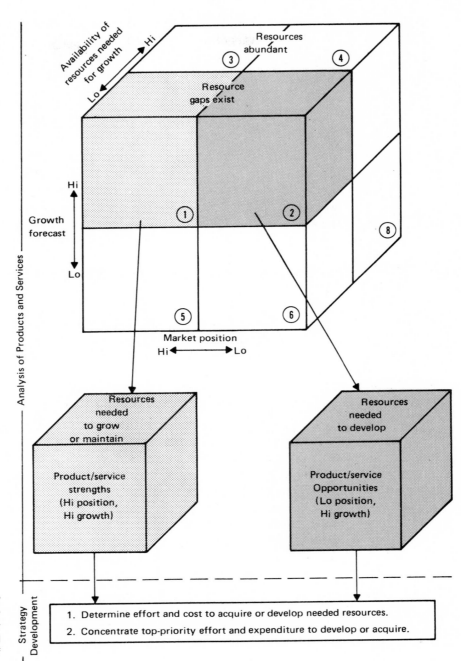

Availability of
resources needed
for growth

Hi
Lo

Resources
abundant

③ ④

Resource
gaps exist

Hi

Growth
forecast

Lo

① ②

⑧

⑤ ⑥

Market position
Hi ◄──────► Lo

Analysis of Products and Services

Resources
needed
to grow
or maintain

Product/service
strengths
(Hi position,
Hi growth)

Resources
needed
to develop

Product/service
Opportunities
(Lo position,
Hi growth)

Strategy
Development

1. Determine effort and cost to acquire or develop needed resources.

2. Concentrate top-priority effort and expenditure to develop or acquire.

FIGURE 7
The process of strategy
formulation for
maintenance and
development of
strengths.

tiveness as well.[4] A simple high-low classification is all that we recommend at this point in the analysis. Later we will describe a simple technique for making a finer classification by ranking the multiple entries in a single cell or in the whole matrix.

The third dimension of the cube subdivides the products or services further, on the basis of the availability of the resources — structural, human, and technological — needed to support each of the products, now or in the future. Again we use a two-way classification, high and low, indicating either abundance or a significant resource gap.

At this point we will not examine products for which *all* resources are abundant (cells 3 and 4 in the figure), nor the low-growth products in cells 5, 6, 7, and 8. Instead, we will select cells 1 and 2 for further analysis. This forces us to concentrate our attention on the major product *strengths* (high position and high growth) and *opportunities* (low position and high growth), where we have identified resource gaps which stand in the way of developing our opportunities or maintaining our strengths. Figure 7 shows these two cells removed from the original matrix. We will return to these shortly.

The other cells cannot be ignored, of course. In cells 5 and 7 (hidden in the figure) are those products which are not likely to contribute much more in the future than they do now, and may actually decline in importance. They do play a major role in the overall strategy, since — because of high market position — they may be prime sources of cash flow to support the growth needs in other areas. Your "dogs" or losers should not be in these cells, but should be relegated to cells 6 and 8. Give them special critical attention with a view to phasing them out and freeing for better use elsewhere the resources they now demand.

The actions taken on products in the low-growth regions of this matrix are critical in determining whether or not the organization has a balanced program of change (see Unit 6). The growth strategy should not be based on blind loyalty to the existing product scope, which fails to recognize the limits on available management re-

---

[4]This type of matrix appears frequently, with variations, in the literature on planning. For examples of its use, see Frank T. Paine and William Naumes, *Strategy and Policy Formation* (Philadelphia: W. B. Saunders Co., 1974), p. 157; *Business Week,* p. 49, April 28, 1975; and Rothschild, op. cit.

sources and financing as the business grows. Indeed, it is to the products in these cells that management should look first for the needed resources, identified in cells 1 and 2, to exploit the product opportunities and strengths. Some part of the abundant resources in cells 3 and 4 may also be available for reallocation to the products in cells 1 and 2. However, this could weaken the very products which now represent your strongest assets, those which are strengths and opportunities for which you do *not* need to be concerned about the resources to support or exploit them, at least for the present.

Cells 1 and 2 in Fig. 7 summarize the organization's major strengths, opportunities, and resource needs, which are the basis for strategy formulation. Once the critical resource gaps are identified, the strategy development process consists of determining the effort and cost required to develop or acquire the needed support, and— finally and most importantly—concentrating and maintaining top-priority effort on these tasks.

The strategy which emerges from the above process ensures that your attention is directed first to the preservation and development of the organization's delivery strengths, and second to the major obstacles standing in the way of achieving those ends. In the event there are not enough resources to go around, the foregoing analysis pinpoints the product or service areas from which presently allocated resources might be diverted.

An example of sound strategic planning which illustrates this process is offered by the semiconductor products business of the General Electric Company. Having identified a number of very attractive high-growth, but low-position, "opportunities" for the future, that company firmly refused to become involved. The resource gaps—large capital investment, heavy working capital requirements, and tremendous demands on technical effort caused by rapid product obsolescence—were so formidable that the sound strategy was to forego many major growth opportunities.

In commenting to a group of security analysts,[5] the head of the semiconductor operation stated:

" " *... By staying out of these high-risk markets, we can put more substantial resources into the ... end of the product*

---

[5]Quoted in *The General Electric Investor,* p. 11, Winter 1977.

spectrum where we have the leadership, the technology, and the market position. . . . By this strategy we have dramatically raised the earning power . . . of the business. **" "**

Referring to this as a strategy of "controlled growth in those segments of the market where we have the greatest product and marketing strengths," he stated that the business was approaching future opportunities by "focusing its resources." In terms of the matrix in Fig. 7, the focusing effect comes from allocating to products in cells 1 and 3 some of the resources that otherwise would continue to be devoted to cell 4 products, and by diverting growth funds from attractive opportunities in cell 2 to a few carefully selected products in cell 1.

Many other examples of the result of the type of thinking we have presented here, or the lack of it, appear in *Business Week*'s section on corporate strategies.

FUNCTIONAL SUPPORT STRATEGY

We establish for each of the functions in the organization a 2x2 matrix as shown in Fig. 8. This time the dimensions are strength and need. Again we divide the functional and subfunctional resources and capabilities into "high" and "low" according to their *strength* and their *need*. It is immediately apparent that the high-need-low-strength cell could be filled, without further analysis, by the entries you have made in the resource gap matrices of Fig. 7. We urge, however that when you use Fig. 8 you independently make the entries in all four cells without referring to your product strategy matrices. In other words, focus your attention on the strengths of the function as

FIGURE 8
The need-strength matrix for development of functional support strategy.

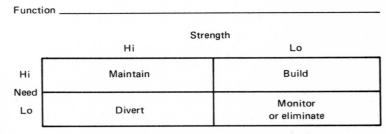

(Entries are specific subfunctions, resources and capabilities.)

objectively as you can—admittedly a difficult task if you are the manager of that function or of one of its subfunctions.

When you have finished both processes (Figs. 7 and 8), it will be instructive to compare the results. If, for example, your finance, manufacturing, or any other function is viewed in its proper role of supporting product strategy, rather than serving primarily its own ends and interests, the major resource needs identified in Fig. 7 should bear a close correspondence to those in the high-need–low-strength cell of Fig. 8. If they do not correspond, for whatever reason, you must reconcile the difference.

To illustrate, let's say that a major product opportunity (see Fig. 7) shows as one of its critical resource needs "a field sales force highly trained in industrial sales." If that same need does not appear in the "build" cell of Fig. 8 in the marketing matrix (or if it appears in some other cell), differing perceptions about the strength of, or the need for, the industrial sales force capability are indicated. This sometimes happens when more than one department is involved in preparing the two matrices. If you find substantial discrepancies, you must set up interdepartmental discussions to reconcile them. If you are in a function other than marketing, it will help if you team up with a colleague in the marketing (or direct delivery) arm of your organization when you apply these techniques, using the exercises which follow.[6]

The remaining cells in Fig. 8 include those labeled "maintain" (high-strength–high-need) and "divert" (high-strength–low-need). These two in particular deserve a few words of explanation. The "divert" cell implies a strategy of reallocating strengths which are not being utilized to an area where there are major resource gaps. Frequently a way can be found to plug such gaps at a lower cost than by other more obvious means, such as acquisition from outside the organization. Examination of this cell can, in effect, change your estimate of both the cost and the availability of a needed resource. (Interfunctional rivalry, protectiveness, or merely functional myopia often stands in the way of a serious and objective effort to effect this change.)

---

[6]The *Leader's Manual* accompanying this series describes a meeting format wherein larger groups can be used to reach consensus or agreement on such matters, and can construct the matrices themselves.

The "monitor or eliminate" cell may contain some entries representing a token effort by the organization to keep abreast of technology or other developments which apparently are currently making no real contribution. In this category we could place the minor efforts that energy-related businesses were putting into the development of knowledge and skills in using solar power up until a few years ago. The importance of monitoring the need for allocation of funds and manpower to that particular field is now quite obvious. Other entries in the low-need-low-strength cell may be vestigial activities no longer needed nor contributing to the health of the organization. The sooner these are eliminated and the effort put into more important things, the better.

THE QUANTIFI-CATION OF JUDGMENT

You have now identified the products and the resources whose strengths you need to maintain or build, and some others which you can allow to dissipate or which you should forcibly prune to keep them from draining strength from other areas. Many organizations find at this point that they are blessed with more opportunities than they can handle, or that they need more resources than they can expect realistically to develop, or both. To convert this welter of information into *strategy,* and finally into sound organizational objectives, you need a *selection process* that will be more discriminating than the rough "high-low" classification scheme we have used in the preceding analysis. Although this scheme serves to demonstrate the process and perhaps to separate the sheep from the goats, it does not ensure that a goat has not slipped into the fold nor that a sheep has not been likewise misplaced. (Much more important than the selection process itself, of course, is the organizational discipline and control which ensure that soundly conceived and selected strategy is *followed.*)

We do not wish to overemphasize the necessity for quantification. MBO has already suffered too much from the naive notion that everything worthwhile must be capable of being expressed in numbers. This has had the unintended effect of downgrading the importance of judgment in the decision-making process. In fact, judgment must play a major role even in the most *quantifiable* decisions. For example, ranking the value of a series of investment proposals may be based on a very precisely calculated discounted rate of return for each project proposed. However, the decision about which proposal should have top priority must be based on the judgment of relative risks of failure, uncertainties in cost and investment assumptions, and the magnitudes of the cash flows involved, as well as the discounted return rate itself.

The criteria for ranking sets of projects, products, or organizational resources in terms of such attributes as value, cost, probability of success, and importance are of course tremendously diverse. The example we have used (a set of investment proposals) may contain research laboratory facilities which will bear fruit many years in the future, a major investment to improve the safety and security of the plant, several urgent redesign projects to reduce costs immediately, and the facilities to produce a new product to replace an obsolescent one over a period of several years. Under such circumstances, a heavy dose of judgment is obviously needed to place the various proposals in priority order. Ranking is a necessary procedure if resources are limited, if the organization uses "zero-base" budgeting, or if you simply want to be as confident as possible that the entries in the matrices of Figs. 7 and 8 are placed in the most appropriate cells.

A tool which can facilitate the judgmental decision making required in such situations is the method of paired comparisons. In this procedure, each member of a group of n items is compared separately with each of the remaining items until all of the possible comparisons are made, $[n(n-1)/2]$ in all. No "ties" are allowed. After all these forced-choice comparisons are made, each item is awarded a number of points equal to the number of times it was chosen over the others with which it was compared. Finally, the items are ranked in decreasing order of points awarded. This method is especially useful in ranking items in sets for which n is greater than 10.[7] For

---

[7] Paired comparisons in small sets often result in apparent inconsistencies or "intransitivities" which make the results difficult to interpret. For example, in a set of three items—vanilla, chocolate, and strawberry—it is entirely possible although unlikely, for the choices to be vanilla over chocolate, strawberry over vanilla, and chocolate over strawberry. This would result in a three-way tie for the top rank, while a more likely (and transitive) series of choices might be vanilla over chocolate, chocolate over strawberry, and vanilla over strawberry, in which case the rank order becomes vanilla (2 points), chocolate (1 point), and strawberry (no points). In large sets a limited number of inconsistencies will not affect the rankings unduly. If a large amount of such ambivalence does exist, it is often the result of interfunctional conflict or protectiveness in the organization. This issue must obviously be resolved before the ranking process can be carried out in a systematic manner.

smaller sets, the items can usually be ranked equally well by inspection, with the paired comparisons made only on those items where the members of a group disagree on the order, or when there are a number of items (usually those intermediate in rank) which appear "too close to call."

The above ranking procedure is useful at various points in the strategic planning process when considering such matters as:

> The relative importance of client group claims on the organization
>
> The contributions of the various organizational strengths or product opportunities identified
>
> The potentially harmful effects of weaknesses and resource gaps
>
> The probabilities of success of various strategic postures, product innovations, cost-reduction projects, etc.
>
> Verifying the allocation of a series of products, needs, or strengths between the "high" and "low" cells of a matrix, or selecting a limited number of items in a cell for more detailed analysis

This procedure is also useful in ranking the importance of the organizational objectives which follow from the strategic posture we have developed in this unit. We will discuss objectives further in Unit 8. But before we leave the subject of strategy, a few examples will help to illustrate how the strategic planning process has been carried out (or ignored) by organizations in the past.

Probably the best example of the imaginative use of latent strengths as a basis for future opportunities and service is the banking industry's surge to the forefront of the credit card market. Recognizing the profitability of its consumer credit operations, the industry put to work the tremendous unused potential of its computer capacity to handle the required volume of transactions at low cost. By providing an integrated service, the banks changed the broad-use credit card from a luxury of the jet set into a fixture of practically every middle-class family.

Strategic planning is hardly a new or unknown activity, and it would not be difficult to find other outstanding examples of its application. However, it is probably more instructive to look at the other side of the coin—cases involving misapplication of the principles. Too numerous to mention are the acquisitions made by firms which established a growth strategy concerned primarily with increased earnings per share of stock, but failed to consider the strengths needed for success in the newly acquired fields.

The recent misadventures of Westinghouse Electric with its record club, educational publishing, and other acquired ventures provide an example. The recovery of that company—upon getting rid of a number of these recent acquisitions—is an equally good example of recognition of the need for strategic thinking. Not content to confine its attention to the new businesses, management applied the same analysis to its older established activities and subsequently sold its household appliance business, which was not contributing to the firm's future in proportion to the managerial and other efforts being applied to it.

Many of these ventures were highly competitive in nature as well as totally foreign to the management skills of the firms involved. The frequent result was either an excessive reliance on imported managers, with concomitant failure to establish control of the new businesses, or a misguided faith in the ability of a good manager to "manage anything." Such an assumption of universal strength has led not only to disappointing business results but to the premature end of many a promising management career as well.

Business firms are not the only organizations that are often guilty of ignoring or misusing the principles of sound strategic think-

"Mine was the sin of overdiversification."

ing. A Community Development Corporation, funded by the federal Office of Equal Opportunity to serve a major Southeastern city and its rural environs, exhibited great skill in mobilizing citizen groups behind such ventures as regional medical clinics, community water purification and distribution systems, and day-care centers. Encouraged by these successes, the steering committee decided to enter several commercial manufacturing ventures. The mission of the corporation, which had originally been community betterment, became oriented more toward economic than toward social ends. While the rationale was the creation of employment in the community, the business ventures chosen—a furniture manufacturing firm, an electronic assembly operation, and a paper container plant, among others—required high capital investment and created few additional jobs. The analysis of proposed new ventures and the monitoring of those selected for implementation were done by a group whose strengths, while impressive in the accomplishment of the original social service mission, were inadequate to the task when the mission became diffused. Some of these ventures were abandoned after several years, and the management effort concentrated on those remaining. The agency is now regaining its earlier well-deserved reputation with the funding source and, more importantly, is strengthening its impact on the community.

In all such cases, we find the mission preceding the analysis, which should have come first, and often the mission itself is ignored in favor of highly attractive objectives of the type deplored by Tavel (see Unit 4). These cases reflect a common tendency to attempt an answer to the question "Where are we going?" without giving sufficient thought to "Why are we here?" and "Who are we?" The pervasiveness of this inverted logic is even greater in the personal strategies of countless managers and professionals who give little thought to the latter two questions—until the all-too-frequent mid-career identity crisis occurs.

You are now in a position to set objectives for your organization—objectives that reflect the detailed analysis we have just completed, not merely high-sounding generalizations or impossible dreams. Based on strategies which (1) lead from strength and (2) concentrate those strengths where they can do the most good, they provide a much more precise and realistic answer to the question "Where are we going?" The nature of organizational objectives will be discussed further in Unit 8.

EXERCISE 7 1. Referring to Fig. 7, enter in the four cells of a 2x2 position-growth matrix the products or services of your organization (or of yourself as an individual). Taking one entry from either the high-position–high-growth cell or the low-position-high-growth cell, complete the availability analysis and identify the critical resource gaps. Express the result of your analysis as a strategy statement which deploys resources and makes possible the achievement of appropriate objectives.

2. Referring to Fig. 8, select a function meaningful to your organization (see Table 2 or your results from Exercise 5 as a refresher), and make entries appropriate for all four cells of the need-strength matrix. Express at least one strategy statement in each of the four categories (maintain, build, divert, and monitor).

3. Consider the following list of possible self-improvement projects you might undertake or request to further your career or otherwise influence your future. Rank them by the method of paired comparisons according to their value to you at this point in your career:

A college-level course in your functional specialty

A lateral assignment in another function

A voluntary committee chairmanship in a community activity such as the United Fund

A year's sabbatical to do advanced study in your specialty

An overseas assignment with your firm

Sensitivity training

An arrangement with a career counseling and placement firm

An assignment as assistant to a top-level executive in your firm or agency

Enrollment in a top-quality university executive development program

An extended vacation

Development of a hobby or avocation which will make your retirement years more productive

Employment part-time with a local community college or university as an adjunct faculty member to teach in your field

A staff assignment in your specialty

Attendance at a series of management seminars on human relations

A course in creative writing

A reading program in management or technical periodicals and books

A management position in charge of factory or office workers

A management position in which your subordinates are managers or supervisors

Training in computers and management science

Team building or other group development activities with your associates

Financial or estate planning advice from an investment counselor

Commentary on Exercise 7

1. and 2.   Perhaps you experienced difficulty in transforming the output of the matrix-development processes into statements of strategy. The following two typical statements may be used as models against which you can compare your own results:

❝ *Strategy to capitalize on international trade opportunities will be based on: (1) use of the existing consumer electronic sales offices and sales support facilities in the South American and western European market areas to house and administer the nucleus of an industrial sales force in these two market areas; (2) assistance available from the State Office for Trade Development and the Community College system in training key personnel in shipping and documentation procedures and the necessary foreign language skills; (3) acceleration of engineering and development of the promising pump and control product lines; and (4) staffing of this total effort to the extent possible with personnel to be made available from cutback in the level of effort on the compressor lines.* ❞

❝ *I. Key results area:* Public Responsibility
II. Strategy:

> *While efficiently run, this city administration suffers from a very weak public image as a tight-fisted, hard-nosed, penurious organization with little regard for the well-being and feelings of individual citizens. In the face of the general situation, the police department has made great strides in improving its own image from one of 'brutality' to one of 'helpfulness' as determined by recent polls. A major strategic emphasis for the future will be to utilize the training strengths and techniques developed in the police department or available locally to provide human awareness training for all city employee groups which interface with the public, including sanitation workers, meter readers, welfare and social workers, purchasing agents, and revenue collectors. The city manager and executive staff will also undergo such training to learn the importance of desirable behavior and to enable them to model it in their relations with their employees.* ❞

3. Rank ordering the list of career or personal development possibilities in terms of their value will of course vary depending upon your point on the career path, your own perception of your potential, your aspirations, and in general what your experience has been.

It is almost certain that some of the items at the top of the list may be completely out of reach, while others of lesser value may be readily accomplished. This is no more than a clear demonstration that the mechanical procedures for determining priorities, while an aid to judgment, do not replace it. Indeed, they serve to highlight even more clearly the necessity of good judgment in situations like this.

If you yourself had selected the items making up the list in number 3, your judgment might have consciously or unconsciously weeded out those which had a low probability of success or accomplishment. As it stands, however, you may wish to go back and rank the list in terms of probability or availability. Note that this will call for even more judgment, since you will be forced to consider both value and probability of success, and to combine the two factors to determine the ultimate rank.

You may prefer to fall back on the matrix technique. A 3x3 matrix of value and probability with qualitative "high," "medium," and "low" cells will organize the information and also provide a starting point for a process such as the one in Fig. 7, expanding on the contents of the high-high, high-medium, and medium-high cells:

	Value		
	High	**Medium**	**Low**
Probability of Success or Execution — **High**			
Medium			
Low			

For those of a more quantitative bent or whose decision making is in an area such as capital investment budgeting, which lends itself to numerical analysis, there are techniques for incorporating large numbers of variables, including probability distributions for each, into a single value or range of values for a criterion such as discounted rate of return. See the Bibliography at the end of this volume for sources.

UNIT 8

ORGANIZATIONAL OBJECTIVES

EPILOGUE AND PROLOGUE

Our reasons for deferring the consideration of objectives for your organization until now should be clear. "Where you are going" cannot be intelligently determined until you know precisely where you are, and the process of self-analysis which you have gone through in the preceding units, based on the needs and demands of your organization's clients, should have provided you with the required insights. It should also have made clear to you the options or alternatives available for moving in the most promising or needed directions. These are the strategies. Objectives which follow from this deliberate process become sharply focused commitments as to how far and how fast to move in the desired directions.

The process of strategic thinking as we have implemented it often proves distasteful to the action-oriented manager whose natural tendencies are to get on with the job — to sight a target and shoot for it. Most of us are better suited to so-called convergent thinking. We like to zero in on a course of action, rather than engaging naturally in the broadly divergent[1] thought process advocated here, which *deliberately* thwarts our normal decisive, problem-solving approach. This divergent process, rigorously followed, is a necessary first step in implementing an MBO system which really works. We will spend considerable time in Vol. II on objective setting. However, if we do not first assure ourselves that the objectives meet the real needs and capabilities of the organization, the whole MBO process is robbed of much of its potential as a management system.

This is not to say that *components within an organization* cannot "start with objectives" and implement a strong system of internal planning, feedback, and control. At the working levels in an organization, objectives are often dictated by the situation or by the need to conform with objectives set at higher levels. It is when higher-level objectives are misconceived or converged upon without a strategic planning approach that the MBO system often fails, even when implemented "by the book" at the operating level.

THE LIFE EXPECTANCY OF STRATEGY

It is conceptually sound for a strategy statement to precede the establishment of objectives, for the reasons we have stated. Objectives must be highly dynamic, subject to continual review, refinement, and adjustment. By contrast, strategy, if properly developed, represents a continuing commitment of resources, and of development and deployment of strengths in a consistent direction. A good strategy will need to be changed only when it no longer provides guidance or when there is a major organizational realignment or upheaval.

As an example, a strategy to concentrate resources on the development of a new product and to acquire the strengths necessary to make it the company's chief breadwinner no longer provides a guide when that happy outcome is finally reached (or, unhappily, is eventually found to be clearly out of reach). The appropriate

---

[1]The terms "convergent" and "divergent" are used by authorities in the field of human creativity to describe respectively the narrow, pedestrian thinking which jumps to conclusions that fail to tap the latent "idea-power" of the subconscious mind, and the broad open-ended exploration of a problem and its setting which encourages creative solutions.

strategy then becomes maintenance or phase out, rather than concentration and investment.

A strategy must be periodically reviewed to see whether it is still effective: Is the strategy guiding the allocation of resources in the directions which best exploit the organization's strengths and capitalize on its opportunities? The proper frequency of review is difficult to prescribe for any given organization. The need for a strategy review is signaled by any major change in the environment (social, economic, political or regulatory, technological) or in competitive activity or industry structure, by a change in top management, by the maturing or decline of any major product line, or by the realization that there is no longer a clearly discernible set of objectives which requires or utilizes the deployed resources effectively.

Strategy review is also needed when the action plans required to achieve the organizational objectives prove too costly in terms of the resources necessary to achieve them. If the total cost exceeds the ability of the firm to acquire or allocate the tools to do the job, the statement of organizational purpose may be describing "mission impossible," and the strategy may be correspondingly meaningless. Some opportunities are always out of reach, even to the most affluent firms with the highest support from their claimants. If the organization finds itself facing this kind of problem, it is often the result of a self-perceived mission of being all things to all people, which can lead in turn to a grand strategy long on posture but necessarily short of "muscle."

The process of strategy review is basically the same as that of strategy formulation, retracing the path shown in Fig. 7, with emphasis on changes which may have taken place in perceived competitive strategy, environmental trends, or internal strengths and capabilities.

THE NATURE OF ORGANIZATIONAL OBJECTIVES

The objectives or targets which the business firm or other organization establishes at the overall organizational level will be the basis for the objective-setting process which occurs at all the successively lower levels. This step is therefore especially crucial in the implementation of any MBO program. Its purpose is to energize all the creative and productive resources of the organization, and to direct them toward the highest-priority targets, selected by the process we have described.

You may have noticed that the strategy statements included in the exercise commentary at the end of Unit 7 sounded very much like statements of objectives being considered by the organization. It is permissible and even helpful to flesh out a bare statement of strategic position with illustrative sequential or alternative actions. The chief requirements for transforming such statements into objectives are commitment to timely action and specific wording that avoids ambiguity and allows performance to be measured. We cover fully in Vol. II the criteria and methods necessary for the most effective selection and implementation of the supporting objectives at all organizational levels. But first the operating people in the firm must accept and fully understand the organizational purpose, strategy, and goals.

Understanding will come if top management openly communicates its concerns and priorities and encourages participation in the strategy-formulation process by the key people who will be responsible for carrying out the resulting plans and programs successfully. *Acceptance* is facilitated by lower-level participation in the organizational analysis which composes the strategic planning process. But the major force behind the broad acceptance of and identification with the organization's objectives is the demonstrated concern of top management — by its support of activities needed to implement objectives, by its insistence on continual accounting of progress, and by rewarding that progress appropriately. The performance appraisal process, described in Vol. III, is the most effective tool for communicating top management concern throughout the entire organization.

HOW MUCH PARTICIPA-TION IN STRATEGIC PLANNING? We have stated earlier that strategic planning is appropriate to all levels of organization, including the individual. The basic questions of what strengths are possessed or needed to perform the task, and what long-range plans will use or develop these strengths, are obviously important whatever the level of contribution. It is equally obvious, however, that the strategies of the lower levels have to be constrained and focused by the overall organizational objectives and mission.

Strategic planning for the organization as a whole has been

called "the peculiar province of top management." We strongly suggest that you leave it that way, recognizing of course that the information needed by the corporate planners to develop the concept of mission and strategy for the firm may be buried deep within the organization. This information must be sought out assiduously, and the active contribution of knowledgeable people at whatever level must be cultivated and welcomed. When all the inputs have been obtained, however, the definition of the organization's mission and its major strategic decisions are the responsibility of top management. There must be no sharing or dilution of that crucial responsibility.

We have known organizations in the throes of major programs of change which have solicited full participation by all levels in the development of the basic mission and strategy, in the belief that this was the way to get superior results. The initial response of those at the working level was invariably spirited and appreciative of the opportunity. But these efforts, typically, proceeded through draft after draft and seemed perversely to avoid convergence on anything which would find broad acceptance. The attitude at the working level rapidly became "Tell us what the goals and priorities are and let us get on with the job." There is ample opportunity for participation by all key contributors in the development of supporting strategy and plans for their components, and in their self-controlled pursuit of mutually set objectives, which is the hallmark of MBO. We trust that, whatever your own vantage point may be as you read this—top, middle, or lower level, staff or operating—you will recognize and respect both the unique role played by top management and the necessary involvement of the contributory levels of the organization.

OBJECTIVES OR STANDARDS OF PERFORMANCE?

We spoke earlier and rather disparagingly about objectives set by organizations for themselves without benefit of the strategic thinking that has been the major thrust of this volume. These may in fact fulfill a very useful function—if they provide the organization with standards of excellence or "ideal" performance targets to shoot at. A company may quite properly state a profit target in terms of percentage return on investment, establish a minimum average annual growth rate, or set a productivity improvement goal for its manufacturing function, all without the benefit of strategic planning. It must be recognized by all concerned, however, that without a supportive strategy these are desires only,[2] and that in fact there may be *no* strategy available for achievement of these desires, at least within a short-range planning horizon. We prefer to call such targets "standards of performance" rather than "objectives," although many organizations think of them as "long-range objectives" or "ultimate goals." Once recognized and treated as what they are, they can, if rationally selected, provide a valuable yardstick against which to measure the success of an overall strategy or the cumulative effect of the achievement of shorter-term objectives over a period of time.

There are several bases for the rational selection of long-term performance goals or standards. You may derive them from an analysis of the best previous performance of the organization itself (for example, your best year, or the average of the 3 best years, in recent history). They may be industry-average figures (or the results achieved by your strongest competitor, depending upon your status within your industry or peer group). Similarly, for a profit center in a multiproduct diversified corporation, the performance target may be "company-average" results or any multiple thereof.

Standards may be "engineered," as in the case of output rates for repetitive manual operations, which are synthesized from the times required for the elemental movements comprising the total process. Or they may be based on exceeding some minimum level of performance below which there is evidence that a business or a product has a low probability of survival (e.g., minimum share of a market, or a product quality attribute).

Finally, and probably most frequently, the standard may be an arbitrary (but agreeable both to superior and subordinate) increment of performance above the current level, toward which an improvement trend can be "aimed" and plotted. Such a standard is appropriate in the early stages of a product life cycle when improvement opportunities have not yet been explored, or in the early phases of an MBO implementation program when an organization's skills in objective setting are at a rudimentary level.

---

[2]We rule out standards which simply state the level of performance which the organization is already achieving and which can make a travesty of the whole MBO process.

In Vol. II we will return to the subjects of standards and objectives, and will cover them much more thoroughly. But in Unit 9, before we leave the strategic planning process, we will examine these concepts in the context of a small component in a manufacturing operation and the job of the manager of that operation.

EXERCISE 8   Exercises in the establishment of organizational or component objectives are best left to be done in connection with the study of objectives in the next volume. However, as a project in strategic planning at the personal level, we suggest that you follow the process depicted in Fig. 5 for your own job:

> List the pertinent capabilities, attributes, and contributions related to your job.

Compare them with the needs of your claimants, with your own needs as an organic system, with the qualifications of your competitors in the field in which you work, and with what the changing environment will demand.

Use the need-strength matrix to identify strategies for the present and the future.

Develop career objectives based on your resource allocations and priorities.

Finally, compare these objectives with those you visualized for yourself prior to doing this strategic self-analysis.

Commentary on Exercise 8

It is not necessary that the objectives you set for yourself after this exercise turn out to be significantly different from those which you have cherished, if you have had a clear and soundly based idea of where you are heading all along. However, the process should have given you an increased appreciation for the amount and nature of concentrated effort, time, and other resources needed to achieve those objectives, even if it did not lead you to change them significantly.

UNIT 9

STRATEGY AT THE INDIVIDUAL LEVEL

THE JOB DESCRIPTION

Strategy at the corporate level, no matter how well thought out, will accomplish little if not supported by and incorporated into the thinking of the working levels of the organization. The vehicle for making the individual an instrument of corporate strategy is the *job description*—a detailed statement of the purpose and scope of each key position. The preparation of such a statement is represented on the MBO flowchart (Fig. 1) by the series of process steps designated as the determination of responsibilities and indicators or criteria of success, and the setting of levels or standards of ideal or exemplary performance. These steps precede the setting of individual objectives and are just as important a part of the preliminary work necessary for an effective MBO system as is the

149

corporate-level strategy making we have discussed in the previous units.[1]

A job description is not regarded in most organizations as a statement or an instrument of strategic dimensions. It usually consists of a simple listing of the duties assigned to the position. It serves primarily as a tool for evaluating the salary range for the position, and less frequently as a checklist for occasional review by the incumbent or the boss to assure that all the bases are being covered. To convert such a listing into a statement of strategic proportions is not a difficult or complicated task, although the document itself almost certainly will be more lengthy than the usual job description and will take more time and thought to prepare. Its length and the effort spent, however, will pay off in greatly increased usefulness—in orienting a new employee to the position, in assuring maximum impact of the position on company goals, and especially in preparing sound objectives and measuring performance.

An example of such a document, covering a position with managerial and technical responsibilities, is shown as Fig. 9. It is an actual example, slightly paraphrased, of a position statement prepared by the manager of the newly formed production engineering section of a major producer of plastic materials. The manager wrote it for his own education and as a working document for him and his supervisor to review during the early phases of his new career. These purposes will help to explain its extraordinary length and detail (it is somewhat abridged here), which are more than would be required for the usual uses to which job descriptions are put. In the early phases of an MBO system, however, the length and detail shown here may be quite appropriate and even necessary to assure full definition of jobs and their relationships with each other and to the overall mission.

A thorough reading of the model document of Fig. 9 will clarify the difference between this approach and the more conventional job description. Part I, the mission statement for the manager and

---

[1]Starting point C on Fig. 1 suggests that an individual who wants to test the operation of the MBO process without involving the rest of the organization may do so by following these steps and proceeding to the establishment of individual objectives, plans, and self-measurement. You may wish to take this approach in deciding whether to introduce MBO into your organization or to influence your associates to do so. Doing Exercise 9 is a good way to get started.

TITLE:	Manager of Production Engineering	DATE: 2/21/__
DIVISION:	Manufacturing	
RESPONSIBLE TO:	Plant Manager	LOCATION: Houston

I. Purpose

The manager of production engineering is accountable to the plant manager. The section is responsible for providing and maintaining manufacturing facilities and processes for production of new and existing products at optimum cost and quality levels.

The section is a vital link in the prompt transfer of newly engineered products into full-scale production and is a major contributor to the company's reputation as a responsive, cost-competitive, and quality supplier. It is the company's first line of defense in protecting the safety of employees and customers from the hazards of the production processes and of poorly manufactured products, respectively. It carries primary operating responsibility for the protection and conservation of the impacted environment of the plant.

II. Position Scope and Responsibilities

A. *Functional and Managerial Responsibilities*

Design and install all processing and handling equipment and other manufacturing facilities for new products, expanded production of existing products, environment control, and general plant improvements.

Provide for design of equipment for the above purposes by utilization of engineering resources outside the section, internal or external to the company, whenever the work involved can be done more economically elsewhere.

Revise and standardize existing processes for improved control and quality of all products, and improve labor and machine utilization upon consultation with the manager of industrial engineering and the plant superintendent.

Reduce manufacturing costs by any of the means above, by improvement of material and energy balances, and by service to the manufacturing section to solve production difficulties.

Introduce into plant operation experimental products in cooperation with the engineering division and manufacturing section. Provide for all maintenance and safety services to the Houston plant.

Coordinate and compile plant capacity figures periodically and initiate action to provide necessary increases.

FIGURE 9
Statement of position scope and purpose (pp. 151-54)

Provide estimates of facilities expenditures, manufacturing costs, and other applicable technical data for use by sales and engineering divisions in preliminary evaluations of new products.

Take an active part in plant cost reduction and safety programs, as a member of management.

Maintain an awareness of new technical developments and regulatory requirements within the industry and apply these whenever practicable.

Provide for continuity and growth of plant capability by selecting and developing competent personnel to carry out the work of the section.

B. *Relationship Responsibilities*

Delegate to subordinates the fullest possible measure of authority for decision making and contribution to profits; and provide a climate where employees may discuss their plans and problems, and receive advice and counsel, without relieving them of their decision-making and other operating responsibilities.

Coordinate the resources and efforts of the section with other sections and with the engineering and sales functions by participation in business team and other activities.

Use the functional services and appraisals of staff divisions as their concentration and specialization upon functional aspects enable them to provide such aid.

Make fullest practicable use of informal "channels of contact" to supplement channels shown on the organization chart, and encourage other members of management to do likewise.

III. Position Authority and Reservations of Decision-Making Authority

Standard Practice Instruction PE-4, entitled "Delegation of Authority," establishes reservations of decision-making authority from the manager and subordinates.

The manager has the authority and responsibility to make recommendations as to subject matter on which decision-making authority has been reserved, to secure decisions thereon, and to take appropriate action thereafter.

IV. Criteria and Measures of Performance for the Position

The criteria and measures of successful performance by the manager of production engineering will include the following items.

A. Effectiveness of activities to provide required production facilities for new and existing products, as measured by:

    1. Thoroughness of periodic audit of future needs, and changes in effective plant capacity figures

    2. Extent of lost business because of late facilities installation*

    3. Success of toll production operations when required

    4. Reduction of overtime and/or addition of capacity by cycle, utilization, and yield studies*

    5. Adherence to engineering and environmental standards of quality in production of new products

B. Effectiveness and timeliness of cost reduction efforts, as measured by:

    1. The percentage of actual and budgeted total cost reduction achievement contributed by the production engineering group*

    2. Specific improvements in yield, spoilage, manufacturing cycle, and labor and machine utilization obtained through production engineering activities*

    3. Reduction in utilities consumption and maintenance costs achieved by engineering improvements*

    4. General extent of participation of the group in cost-reduction program activities

    5. Long-term trend in planned production cost levels for all products

C. Effectiveness of maintenance and plant engineering services, as outlined in the position responsibilities and measured by:

    1. Reduction in machine breakdown time*

    2. Effectiveness of cost control against budgets*

    3. Performance against established preventive maintenance inspection programs and parts inventory limits*

    4. Action in cases of emergency breakdown

    5. Coordination of maintenance activities with production schedules

    6. Anticipation of need for changes in and additions to utilities and services to the plant

    7. Operating difficulties encountered in new equipment, and the effectiveness in elimination

    8. Control of costs in connection with plant appropriations*

    9. Labor and space utilization efficiencies achieved by sound design and drafting

    10. Status of labor relations in the maintenance area

[In the original, measures of each of the following criteria were also present. These measures are eliminated here for brevity, but some of them are the subject of Exercise 9, number 5.]

D. Effectiveness of quality-improvement activities

E. Quality of service provided to other sections and to management, in capital budgeting, production cost estimating, facilities design and layout, and other service responsibilities

F. Effectiveness and extent of participation in professional activities and others involving assimilation and adoption of new engineering knowledge and techniques

G. Effectiveness of personnel selection and development, including delegation of responsibility and authority

H. Effectiveness of control and use of assigned financial and other available resources in the company

I. Quality and timeliness of decisions and action on all responsibilities, including recommendations where decision-making authority is reserved

J. Thoroughness of hazard analyses conducted on all products and processes, and effectiveness of design work in reducing safety hazards to employees and customers

*Numerical standards of excellence based on current conditions and needs will be set and maintained until revision is indicated. Review will be annual.

---

the component, clearly establishes the contributions of the component to the whole. Part II resembles the content of most job descriptions in its listing of the responsibilities and duties of the job-holder, with the addition of specific references to the leadership and relationship responsibilities peculiar to any management position. A number of statements are included, however, which add a truly strategic dimension to what would otherwise be a rather sterile recitation of duties and tasks. (Refer to Exercise 9, number 3, for more on this.) Part III puts "teeth" into the job by affirming the decision-making authority of the position. Finally, Part IV specifies the wide range of measurements which may be used in assessing the performance of the operation and of its manager, and identifies those (the starred items) to which nonjudgmental standards of excellence can most readily be applied.

A final word on the usage of the job description. It is obviously impractical to change the document every time the short-term priorities of the job change. These changes do occur, however, and it is quite likely that in any future 3- or 6-month period the full effort of the employee may be required on only two or three of the many responsibilities listed. The job description must be used as a very dynamic tool, with continually shifting weights assigned to its various activities. This is especially important to the individual when the manager uses it as the basis for conducting progress reviews or overall performance appraisals. Job responsibilities neglected by design because they were below the "cut-off" during the period reviewed obviously should be recognized as such.

With the strategic preliminaries completed at both the organizational and individual levels, we will be ready in the next volume to explore the business of objective setting, and the action planning which is an inseparable part of that process. But first, it is well to recall Peter Drucker's warning that sooner or later everything in the planning domain "degenerates into work." If you haven't already discovered that as you progressed through this volume, it is high time that you roll up your sleeves and go to work seriously on Exercise 9 in preparation for the implementation phase of your MBO program.

EXERCISE 9   1.   Starting with your present job description if you have one—or from scratch if you don't—prepare a statement along the general lines of Fig. 9 containing (1) the mission or purpose of the job as it relates to the organizational mission, (2) the scope of job responsibilities in a form which emphasizes your personal strategy (see Exercise 8), and (3) the criteria and measurements of performance on the job.

2. For those criteria of performance in your own job which lend themselves to verifiable measurement, suggest standards representing the
ultimate level of excellence you feel attainable by a superior performer.
(See the starred items in Part IV of Fig. 9 for examples.)

3. Review Parts II and III of Fig. 9. Underline or otherwise identify the portions which in your opinion reflect *strategic* thinking rather than mere definition of duties and responsibilities.

4. Figure 9 refers to Standard Practice Instruction PE-4 which defines the limits of authority delegated to the position. List the items and the limits you would want to have included in such an instruction pertaining to your own job. Compare this "ideal" with your present limits of authority.

5. Suggest measures of quality, effectiveness, or timeliness which you feel would be appropriate for criteria G, H, and I in Part IV of Fig. 9. Star those measures to which you would apply numerical standards of excellence.

Commentary on Exercise 9

1. and 2.   We suggest that you start by comparing your effort with Fig. 9. A better test, of course, is a review by your boss or a mutual critique with an associate. The outcome of greatest value, in the final analysis, is the insight which you may have gained about your job. MBO can help to give a sense of purpose to individuals, but it will be much more effective from the start if they already have that insight.

3.   Some of the strategic thinking found in a careful reading of Fig. 9 reflects:

Maintenance of a "lean" organization with use of outside help to handle overloads

A posture of helpfulness in which several types of services are offered to other components

A corresponding posture of recognition that some of the strengths which the component needs are best located elsewhere and drawn upon when needed, rather than duplicated

A continuing surveillance of trends in utilizing productive capacity so that prompt action can be taken (This also indicates a fairly healthy degree of skepticism and an unwillingness to rely totally on sales forecasts to signal approaching problems.)

Recognition of the need for monitoring the environment for technological changes which might affect the company

A strong management development emphasis in the component

A strong "systems" orientation, in which the component subscribes to an integrative team approach to business and product problems

A willingness to exercise an "initiating" or "gadfly" responsibility to obtain decisions in areas where authority to act has been reserved or withheld

Encouragement of full use of the informal channels of communication, rather than considering the formal organization structure as the determinant

4.   Many restrictions of authority are to be found in standard practice instructions or written policies which have no reference to your position in particular. Some are so obvious or unrelated as to require no documentation (for example, the authority to approve a national union contract). Others, however, might well be collected and put with your job description for ready reference.

Some of the limits of authority which any manager might expect to test frequently are:

Monetary limits on approval of capital appropriation authorizations, purchase orders, contracts, hiring of outside consultants, charitable contributions, and other cash outlays

Approval to hire within budgeted limits

Approval to take disciplinary action toward subordinates, including firings

Approval of salary increases, bonuses, promotions, transfers, deferral of vacations, extended sick leave, etc.

Approval to add new positions or otherwise change the organization structure

Approval of travel to conventions, conferences, and training activities for self and employees

Approval to make speeches, provide press releases, or otherwise represent the company to outsiders

Approval to spend budgeted funds, either discretionary or "earmarked," for purposes not previously planned or approved

Proposing to your boss a written agreement covering these and other items may be especially helpful if you are in a situation where you are required constantly to check with the boss before taking action on anything. The existence of a written agreement provides a degree of security which may help to make the relationship more trusting, in time.

5. These all are areas of performance which have been considered by many managers to be "unmeasurable," and are often omitted from MBO measurement systems for this reason. There are, however, a number of measurements you can apply—though it is true that most of these areas do not lend themselves readily to numerical standard setting. More often, the measurement consists of observation of some specific instance (often called a "critical incident") which reflects the desired type of behavior.

We will have much more to say about measurement problems and solutions in Vols. II and III. For now, here are some of the measurements that appeared in the unabridged "position scope statement" for the manager of production engineering (the starred items may become numerical standards):

G. Effectiveness of personnel selection and development, including delegation of responsibility and authority, measured by:

1. Caliber of personnel added to the group, as determined by peer ratings; expressions of confidence in the group by other managers

2. Thoroughness of performance appraisals, personnel development plans, and evidence of joint career planning between manager and employee

3. Degree of participation and cooperation of production engineering personnel in broader business projects and activities

4. Extent of independence of section activity from the physical presence of the manager

5. Degree of availability of the manager for long-range thinking and broad-gauge matters not involving day-to-day activities of the section

6. Latitude given for—and insistence on—decision making by employees

7. Recognition of substandard areas of performance and actions taken to correct

8. Frequency of consideration of employees of the section for transfer or promotion by other managers, and transfers accomplished*

H. Effectiveness of control and use of assigned financial and other available resources in the company, measured by:

1. Adequacy of budget recommendations in relation to actual requirements of the business

2. Control of expenditures against variable budget*

3. Percentage of projects successfully completed to planned standards of performance*

4. Effectiveness of use of plant experimental facilities, office pool, company staff advisory resources, and others as required

5. Recognition of projects having low probability of success and action taken to close them out

I. Quality and timeliness of decisions and action on all responsibilities, including recommendations where decision-making authority is reserved, measured by:

1. Specific instances of timely decision making

2. Overall "batting average" on major decisions

3. Performance against a standing list of "pending major decisions"

4. Quality of recommendations in position papers, proposals, and other communications

5. Specific instances of effort made to obtain decisions, and action taken on such recommendations

Your own job situation may have suggested other criteria not included above. We hope you included at least a few that you might have considered "unmeasurable" before reading this volume.

BIBLIOGRAPHY

Literature abounds in strategic planning and all of its elements. The following list will provide a good starting point for further reading and specialization. Most of the references provide additional bibliographies of their own, which are extensive but much less selective. The authors—academicians, consultants, and practicing managers—represent a wide spectrum of viewpoints.

Ackoff, Russell L.: *A Concept of Corporate Planning* (New York: Wiley-Interscience, 1970).

Brief and light in weight, but heavy with wisdom in the form of statements like the following, which should be mounted on the wall in front of every planner: "A plan is not the final product of the planning process; it is an interim report," and "The principal value of planning does not lie in the plans that it produces, but in the process of producing them." Also stresses conceptual and mathematical modeling as means of helping the manager utilize available data most effectively.

Andrews, Kenneth R.: *The Concept of Corporate Strategy* (Homewood, Ill: Dow Jones-Irwin, Inc., 1971).

A handbook for strategists, this fairly brief treatment nevertheless discusses strategy in much more detail than we have been able to do in this series. Of special interest are the discussions of criteria for evaluating strategy and of the organization's changing environment.

Drucker, Peter F.: *Management: Tasks, Responsibilities, Practices* (New York: Harper & Row, 1973).

This book has a way of appearing on everyone's bibliography no matter what the topic. However, for those involved in implementing, formulating, or just thinking out organizational strategy, the whole book is "must" reading. Convince yourself by sampling Chap. 7 on mission and purpose and Chap. 10 on strategic planning, "the entrepreneurial skill."

Hertz, David B.: "Risk Analysis in Capital Investment," *Harvard Business Review,* vol. 42, no. 1, pp. 95-106, January-February 1964.

A technique for evaluating and comparing the relative worth of a number of capital investment or product development decisions, incorporating an evaluation of the uncertainties inherent in the data used for calculation. This article provides a useful model which may be applied to other types of analysis as well.

Kahn, Herman, and B. Bruce-Biggs: *Things to Come: Thinking about the Seventies and Eighties* (New York: Macmillan, 1972).

A useful introduction to futurology by the director and a staff historian of the Hudson Institute. Establishes three alternative "surprise-free" projections or scenarios for the future of the United States. Since we are already well into the period in question, this book provides a good test of the ability of futurologists to develop useful projections. There are also chapters on technological forecasting in both a military and a social context.

Lakein, Alan: *How to Get Control of Your Time and Your Life* (New York: Signet Books, 1973).

A book which fills a much-needed function in the literature of time management, that of stressing the value of personal motivation in the successful time management effort and the value of the self-analysis which arouses the motivation. These are essential prerequisites of any successful personal time management or strategic planning process.

MacKenzie, R. Alec: *The Time Trap: Managing Your Way Out* (New York: AMACOM, 1972).

An excellent source of methods, tips, and techniques for saving time, including a concise but excellent treatment of the mysteries and difficulties of delegation.

Paine, Frank T., and William Naumes: *Strategy and Policy Formation* (Philadelphia: W. B. Saunders Co., 1974).

An integrative approach incorporating management science techniques. Of special value are the chapters on assessment guides and methods. These chapters contain useful material to aid the analyst and strategist in defining the organizational situation.

Rosenberg, Seymour L.: *Self-Analysis of Your Organization* (New York: AMACOM, 1974).

Another framework for analyzing the strengths and weaknesses of your organization in the vital areas of the firm's objectives, its procedures for making decisions, its implementation of decisions, its communication and reporting practices, and its psychic energy level. Written from top management's point of view, this work exposes all levels to the strategic dimensions of planning.

Rothschild, William E.: *Putting It All Together: A Guide to Strategic Thinking* (New York: AMACOM, 1976).

Strategic planning as it is carried out by the General Electric Company, including usage of the strategic decision matrix. This book was written by a practitioner who provides numerous case vignettes and also translates the planning process at all stages for understanding and application by managers in nonprofit organizations.

Steiner, George A.: *Top Management Planning* (New York: Macmillan, 1969).

One of the most extensive treatises on planning, this respected volume is encyclopedic in its coverage of concepts, processes, and tools. For those concerned more with functional than with overall business planning, the areas of marketing, financial, research and development, diversification, and product planning are all covered at length. The concepts of strategy and forecasting and the applicability of quantitative techniques and the computer are also included.

Wheelwright, Steven C., and Spyros Makridakis: *Forecasting Methods for Management* (New York: John Wiley & Sons, Inc., 1973).

A concise description of the many types of quantitative and qualitative forecasting techniques available to managers for use in planning. This work contains helpful material on matching the forecasting method with the situation and the planning horizon for greatest effectiveness.

INDEX

INDEX

Page numbers in *italic* indicate charts or graphs.